# A SHORT HISTORY
# OF THE CHURCH OF ENGLAND

# A·SHORT·HISTORY OF·THE CHURCH·OF·ENGLAND

BY

## THE REV. J. F. KENDALL, M.A.

SOMETIME EXHIBITIONER IN HISTORY, KING'S COLLEGE, CAMBRIDGE

PUBLISHED BY A. & C. BLACK
4, 5 & 6 SOHO SQUARE, LONDON

*First published, with sixteen illustrations in colour and*
*eight in black and white, square demy 8vo., cloth,*
*December, 1910*
*This edition published in the Autumn of 1914*

B1633819
G

# Preface

WHEN in a book of this size one has to deal with so large a subject as that of the history of the Church of England, it is obvious that much must be left untold. For details of the events in the long career of the National Church, the reader must therefore turn to larger works. But behind events there lie always the ideas and ideals which led to them; and it is simply the ideas and ideals that have influenced, or in turn have been influenced by, the National Church in its long continuous life which I have tried to describe.

My hope is that I have so far succeeded in my attempt as to make it possible for my readers to place the facts which they gather from elsewhere in their true perspective, and thus to make their study of the subject of real value to them.

J. F. KENDALL.

*July* 9, 1914.

# Contents

CHAPTER                                                    PAGE

    PREFACE - - - V

  I. EARLY DAYS - - - - - 1

 II. NORMANS AND ANGEVINS - - 24

III. MEDIEVAL STRUGGLES - 43

IV. WYCLIFFE - - - - 61

 V. THE CRY FOR REFORM - - 68

VI. POLITICAL REFORMATION - - 85

VII. CHANGES IN PUBLIC WORSHIP 102

VIII. GRADUAL SETTLEMENT - - 113

IX. A HOUSE DIVIDED - - 131

 X. RESTORATION AND REVOLUTION - - - 147

XI. FOREIGN KINGS AND THEIR WAYS - 160

XII. THE METHODISTS - - 185

XIII. NEW LIFE WITHIN THE CHURCH - - - 193

    INDEX - - - 205

# A SHORT HISTORY OF THE
# CHURCH OF ENGLAND

## CHAPTER I

### EARLY DAYS

OUR earliest knowledge of the people who dwelt
in these islands comes from the records which
the great Roman General Julius Cæsar kept
of his military expeditions. He tells us that he
was led into undertaking the conquest of Britain
because he found that this island was a kind ot
harbour of refuge for the people who disturbed the
peace in the province of Gaul—*i.e.*, roughly speaking, modern France. But although Julius Cæsar
came to England twice, he did not succeed in
conquering it. As a matter of fact the conquest
was not a reality till at least 100 years later, and it
was probably only after Britain had then come to
be a part of the great Roman Empire that the

Christian faith was brought to its people. But by whose enthusiasm this bringing of the Faith came about it is impossible to say. There is an old legend that Joseph of Arimathea came with twelve companions and settled at Glastonbury, and in the ground there planted his staff, which budded and grew into the famous Holy Thorn. That beautiful story, however, is only first heard of many hundred years after S. Joseph was dead. The cause which most likely led to the heathen Britons being taught the faith was an outbreak of bitter persecution which fell upon the Christians in South-Eastern Gaul in the year 177. Just as we read in the New Testament that by reason of the persecution of Stephen, Philip and others were scattered abroad, so, too, in all probability as a result of the persecution at Lyons and Vienne, fugitives fled along the great Roman roads to cross the Channel and hide in Britain, as in an earlier day fugitives from the rule of Julius Cæsar had also done.

But whatever were the means by which the faith was first brought to England, there is no doubt about the fact that the Christian Church was a living influence here by the beginning of the third century, for Tertullian, the great Latin Father who lived at that time, speaks of parts of

Britain not yet reached by the Romans as being subjected to Christ.

A hundred years later comes the story of the death of the man who is believed to have been the first martyr for the Faith in England. This was S. Alban, said to have been a soldier in the Roman Army stationed in Britain, and who in a time of persecution sheltered a Christian teacher and contributed to his escape by lending him his own cloak, and afterwards, on being accused of sharing the faith of the man he had befriended, boldly acknowledged the fact and was beheaded. Though doubt has been thrown upon the truth of this story, there seems to be no real reason why it should not be accepted, for we know that within a hundred years of the date on which S. Alban is said to have died, his memory was lovingly revered in England as that of a martyr.

Ten years after the probable date of S. Alban's death—that is, in the year 314—we have a glimpse of the reality of Church life in Britain due to the fact that, at a Church Council held at Arles in that year, there were present three British Bishops together with a priest and a deacon in attendance upon them. The Council had been summoned mainly to deal with a bitter schism which had

arisen within the Church. It dealt also with
questions with regard to the observance of Easter,
and as to what made a valid baptism. But what
interests us here is not so much what the Council
discussed as the fact that present at it were these
delegates from the Church in Britain.

One other time in the history of this British
Church is also full of interest—namely, the coming
of S. German and S. Lupus to strengthen the
Church in Britain in its attempts to crush heresy.
This heresy had sprung originally out of the noble
efforts of a Briton to raise the standard of life
amongst Christians at Rome and elsewhere. The
man himself came to be called by his friends in
Italy by the Greek word 'Pelagius,' which represented the Welsh word 'Morgan,' meaning born of
the sea. Pelagius, as we may call him, exhorted
all men to nobler living. He was answered that
no higher standard could be reached owing to
human weakness. To this Pelagius replied that
what a man ought to do he could do—that is, he
denied the truth of original sin and the necessity
that men stand in of receiving the grace of God to
live a holy life.

Pelagianism so deeply affected the Church in
Britain that the faithful few were compelled at

last to send to Gaul for help. This took place
about the year 429. In response to their request the
Church in Gaul sent them S. German and S. Lupus,
and these men upon their arrival in Britain not
only successfully dealt with the heresy, but also
rendered signal help in a way altogether unexpected. S. German, who was of noble birth and
who in his younger days had been trained to arms,
found on his arrival in Britain that the British were
being sorely harassed by an incursion of Picts and
Scots from the northern part of the island. His
military knowledge enabled him to dispose the
native forces in such a manner that they won a great
victory. He placed them in ambush on either side
of a narrow valley along which their enemies would
come, and then, when the heathen were well
within the valley, at a signal from S. German,
they suddenly shouted out the Easter cry of
*Alleluia* (for it was Easter-time) and rushed forth
from their concealment. The enemy fled in terror
without so much as striking a blow, but the
Britons were either too feeble or too inexperienced
to follow up their victory, and it was not very long
ere they were destined to suffer again and more
severely still at the hands of the same enemy.

Before the coming of S. German to Britain

the country had ceased to be in any real
sense a province of the Roman Empire, for
troubles of so serious a nature were afflicting
the centre of the Empire that the legions from
the extreme parts of it were being called in
for the purpose of self-defence.  These troubles
arose owing to the fact that vast tribes of people
who had been living beyond the Rhine and the
Danube—that is to say, outside the boundaries of
the Empire—were now crossing the boundaries and
threatening even Rome itself.  The Roman Empire
had always known of the existence of these tribes,
and for many a long year had despised them, regarding their own great army and the Rivers Rhine and
Danube as barriers which could never be broken
through.  But the period in which they had
despised them had been succeeded by a period of
anxiety, and this again by a period when it was
seen that the defences could not be trusted.  It is
said that it was owing to pressure from tribes
dwelling in Siberia that the wild races of Central
Europe began to seek a home within the Roman
boundary.  Whether that is so or not, it is certain
that at almost one and the same time tribes were
crossing the Lower Danube into Turkey and
the Rhine into Belgium and France, and even

finding their way through the Passes of the Alps into Italy. This state of affairs explains two things in our own English history. We can see how natural it was that in a moment of such great danger a province like that of Britain should be left to take care of itself. And we can understand also the coming of the English to Britain. These English formed parts of the numerous races which had been dwelling in Central Europe, and they too, it seems, were being thrust westward, compelled to seek new homes. In fact, the whole Empire of Rome, including the province of Britain, was being overrun at one and the same time by races bearing strange names and speaking strange tongues, but all of them made up of men possessed of a vigour which the people of Rome themselves had long lost. It is from these tribes that the various nations of modern Europe have arisen.

The people that settled in England seem to have consisted mainly of men of three different but closely allied families—Jutes, Saxons and Angles The old chroniclers tell us that it was the Jutes who first obtained a settlement in Britain, and they add that this success was due to treachery on the part of one of the leaders of the Britons—a man named Vortigern, who for his own ends gave the hated invaders the kingdom of Kent. We do not know whether this story is true, but certain it is that not only did the Jutes settle in Kent, but that also within a space of another hundred years there were kingdoms in Sussex, in Wessex (that is, Hampshire, Wiltshire and Berkshire), in Essex, in East Anglia, in Middle England (called Mercia) and in North England (called Northumbria). The Britons resisted the invaders as well as they could, and the more they were driven westward the fiercer did the contest become. As a matter of fact, the English never did conquer Wales, and only subdued Devon and Cornwall in the south-west and Cumberland in the north-west many years after they had made a home for themselves in the main part of the island. In all those western districts the British lived on, though divided by the wedges of Englishfolk which reached to Chester in the north-west and to the Bristol Channel in the south-west.

These English tribes were heathen—fiercely heathen, indeed—and they destroyed almost every sign of Christian worship in England. The Britons took with them into their fastnesses their faith and their worship, but the British Church, cut off in this way from all connection with the Continent

of Europe, not unnaturally lost its power. For a
time it seems to have made an effort to live on
in spite of its isolation, for at Llanwit Major there
was a flourishing college attended at one time by
as many as 2,000 students. But this prosperity did
not continue. The one glorious piece of work which
the British Church might have engaged in—viz.,
the winning of the heathen invader to the Cross,
and thus conquering their conquerors—this they
never attempted.

This work of conversion was done by men
coming from altogether different sources. Some-
where about 200 years after the day when the
English first began to settle in England a young
deacon named Gregory, passing through the
slave-market of Rome, was attracted by the sight
of some fair-haired boys being offered there for
sale. Their fairness stood out in striking contrast to the darker skins of the unhappy captives
from Africa and the East. Gregory asked the slave-
dealer from whence he had got them, and was told
that they had been brought from England where
all the people were heathen. Fired with missionary
zeal Gregory thereupon obtained permission to
come to evangelize the English, and actually
started on his journey. But he was not allowed to

proceed very far, for the people of Rome loved him too well to spare him and insisted upon his return. When, however, some five or six years later Gregory himself became Bishop of Rome, he showed at once that he had not forgotten the English. He ordered his agents to buy such English boys as were being offered anywhere for sale that he might have them trained as evangelists to their own countrymen; but without waiting till such a scheme as that could become fruitful, he sent a friend of his own named Augustine with a large party of companions to carry the message of the Church to the English. It seems that neither Augustine nor his fellow-missionaries were possessed of quite the intrepid spirit that stirred the Bishop, for on the way across France they heard such terrible stories of the ferocity of the English that Augustine was sent back to Rome to ask Gregory to set them free from their task. The Pope bade them not lose heart, telling them that no man who had put his hand to the plough should look back. At the same time he encouraged them by writing letters to influential people on the route, and gave them letters of commendation to King Ethelbert of Kent and to his wife, Queen Bertha. So it came about that at last the mission arrived. The date

was some time soon after Easter in the year 597.
This is one of the notable dates in English history,
for it is the date of the first coming to the English
of that Faith which has done so much to make
English life what it is.

It was in every way natural that Augustine and
his companions should make for Kent. Not only
was it the nearest kingdom to the Continent, but
the Queen Bertha was herself already a Christian,
and Gregory rightly hoped that by her intervention
the strangers might receive a kindly welcome.
Their reception was all that could be desired. The
King listened to Augustine while he spoke of the
' merciful Saviour who had redeemed the world by
His own agony, and had opened the kingdom of
heaven to all believers,' and at the end of the
address told the strangers that the words he had
heard were beautiful indeed but sounded strange,
and he could not be expected to give up at once the
old national gods. He was willing, however, to
give them hospitality in his own capital city, and
to allow them to win his people to their way of
thinking if they could. The new-comers met at
first with marked success. Attracted by the moral
beauty of their lives, many of the Kentishmen
became Christian, and when, within the year, the

King himself came to be baptized, there seemed
no reason why that should not be regarded as
a promise of much further success still.  But with
the increase in the number of converts important
questions of administration arose, and it is clear
from Augustine's method of dealing with them that
he was not quite the man for the work.  Someone
was required possessed of much practical wisdom
and with a power of initiative.  Augustine, however, was not a man of that kind.  He can scarcely
be blamed for that.  Until he was sent to England
he had spent the greater part of his life in a
monastery where the days were governed by
routine and where men get little experience of the
rough and tumble of the outside world.  Now he
was called upon to deal with a people whose
customs and habits were strange to him, and for
whom everything had to be done in the way of
building up a system of Church government and
worship.  Evidently bewildered, he wrote to
Gregory for directions.  He wanted guidance
about the proper distribution of alms, about the
composition of the public service of the Church;
also whether cousins might marry, or whether a
man might marry his stepmother.  The replies he
received bring out in striking relief the practical

ability of the good Pope. Especially interesting is Gregory's advice as to the construction of a service-book for the use of the English converts. There was no reason, he said, why the Roman service should be imposed upon the English people, but if Augustine had come across other usages in Gaul or elsewhere which he thought might be helpful to the English, then he ought certainly to adopt them in pre-ference.

But outwardly all things seemed to be making for the success of the mission. A striking develop-ment took place when Edwin, the King of North-umbria, sought for a wife at the Kentish Court. Ethelbert was by this time dead; so, too, was Augustine. Justus had succeeded Augustine, while in the place of Ethelbert his son Eadbold was reigning, and it was Eadbold's sister Ethel-burga whom Edwin desired to marry. On the advice of Justus, the King at first refused to let his sister be wedded to a heathen, but afterwards gave his permission when Edwin not only promised that the Princess should have full liberty of worship, but that also he and his wise men would be willing to receive instruction in the Christian Faith.

Here was the promise of a great opportunity in

a new part of England. With the Princess went
Paulinus, one of a number of men sent by
Gregory to reinforce the original band, and who
was now consecrated to the Episcopate. The
success which had marked the coming of Augustine
to Kent was repeated in Northern England.
Edwin was baptized on Easter Eve, 627, and very
many of his people with him. But Edwin was a
more important man than the King of Kent. His
kingdom stretched from the Humber to Edin-
burgh (which is Edwin's Burgh) on the north, and
from sea to sea on east and west, whilst beyond
the boundaries of his own kingdom he exercised his
influence on behalf of his new Faith. The people
of Lindsey (Lincolnshire) and of East Anglia were
also made Christian. Then, however, came an
appalling catastrophe. The Christian Britons of
Wales in alliance with the heathen English of
Mercia, or Middle England, made an onslaught on
Edwin, defeated and slew him, and overran his
whole country. Paulinus fled back to Kent with
the widowed Queen and her little children, and
the work which had been so gloriously begun in
Northern England and which had spread so
rapidly seemed to be destroyed at a blow. Before
long, however, the work was revived, but this time

by men of a stronger personal courage than that of Paulinus, and possessed of a more intense personal faith.

Seventy years before the death of Edwin there had settled in Iona, a little island off the western coast of Scotland, a body of Irish monks under the leadership of S. Columba. It is said that Columba was filled with remorse at the thought of the many who had died in a battle for which he had been responsible, and therefore he had left his home to win at least as many souls to the Faith as had been killed in battle. The mission thus founded in Iona became a wonderful centre of evangelizing zeal; the fame of it spread to England; and at the time of Edwin's death it was acting as a harbour of refuge for men who feared Edwin's power. Edwin himself had been at one time an exile in East Anglia, having been dispossessed by his brother-in-law, Ethelfrith, a man of great force of character, but, as Bede described him, a ravening wolf. When Edwin came to his own by the death of Ethelfrith in battle, then Ethelfrith's children in turn were driven into exile, and they found refuge in Iona. Seventeen years one of these children, Oswald by name, remained there. At last came his opportunity. As heir to his father Ethelfrith, and practically as heir to Edwin, for Edwin's little chil-. dren had been taken into Kent with their mother, Oswald fought and won the Battle of Heavenfield, drove out the ravagers of his patrimony, and after that reigned for the space of eight years. He was an ideal Christian King. In him was seen the strength and vigour of his father not lessened but purified by the influence of the Faith he had learned in his years of exile.

One of Oswald's first acts as King was to obtain from Iona missionaries who should do for his subjects what Iona itself had done for him. The man who came, S. Aidan, was soon recognized to be as noble a priest as Oswald was a King. Bede's love for Aidan's memory is revealed again and again in his account of the times. King and Bishop worked hand in hand, the King oftentimes acting as interpreter that his people might the better understand the message. One incident in the life of Oswald may serve as an indication of his character. Dining one day with the Bishop by his side, he was told that many of his subjects, famished with hunger, had collected outside the hall. The King thereupon sent them his own meat, and in addition gave an order that even the silver dish upon which it had been placed should be broken up and the pieces scattered amongst the crowd.

The work of evangelization, in this way so splendidly renewed by Aidan and the others who came from Iona, spread in time beyond the borders of the northern kingdom. As a matter of fact, the different sections of English people owed much more to Iona than they did to Rome so far as the actual work of conversion was concerned. But to have been permanently linked up with Iona rather than with Rome would have been disastrous for the growing Church life of the English people. For though Iona stood for Apostolic fervour, it was rather to Rome that one had to look for statesmanship and education. A young Church needs after it has been founded to be trained and disciplined. It is the glory of Iona that it had a large part in the one; it is very doubtful if it could have done the other. The acceptance of the Roman method of calculating Easter and of other Roman customs rather than those of Iona was agreed to at a great Conference which was held at Whitby in the year 664, when Oswy, a brother of Oswald, was King, and this decision meant, of course, communion with Rome rather than with Iona.

Four years after the date of this Conference

further help came to England from Rome. As a result of a request made by the Kings of Kent and Middle England, the Pope of the time sent a certain Theodore, a Greek, to fill the vacant Archbishopric of Canterbury. This Theodore was a man well fitted both by character and intellect for his arduous post, but he was already at the time very nearly seventy years of age. He lived, however, till he reached the age of ninety, and during that long period of more than twenty years of work he was able to exert an influence for which the Church of England has constant reason to be grateful. Under his wise direction the various Christian communities in England came to be organized into one whole. Large dioceses were, indeed, split up—that was part of Theodore's policy—but all were made to realize that a common bond bound them together. On every side there was political anarchy, but within the Church there was unity. The Archbishop also promoted the division of every diocese into parishes each with its own resident priest, so that the needs of individuals might never be neglected. Moreover, for the better settlement of problems which affected the people of the whole country, he began the practice of summoning all the Bishops to meet him at a common centre, and the people thus witnessed the strange spectacle of Bishops, whose main interest they had thought was the care of souls in their own dioceses, meeting together because conscious that each diocese was, after all, only a part of a larger Church. There can be no doubt that the people laid this lesson to heart and applied it later on to political affairs. English people were first taught to meet in Parliament by seeing their clergy meet in Synods.

By the time that Theodore had done his work the Church of England had obtained the organization and system which has marked it ever since. What remained still to be done was that its teaching should mould the character of the English people. Each part of the country was nominally Christian now, but heathen practices and heathen ideas lived on for many a long day. Yet as time went by one can see how wonderfully the Church did her work. Noble examples of this are to be found in such lives as those of King Edmund of East Anglia and King Alfred of Wessex. In each of these men Christian ideals were worthily fulfilled. Edmund, however, was killed by heathen Danes, suffering death gloriously rather than be false to his Church. To Alfred, on the other hand, was given a wider opportunity.  His story is one of the few that Englishmen know amongst the many that they ought to know.  He gave proof of what his training had been when he placed the Ten Commandments in the forefront of his Code of Laws, and such an action was something much more than an empty form, for those Commandments said amongst other things that all human life was sacred, while the old English customs had said that the murder of any man could be atoned for by the payment of a fine.  So also the working man's weekly day of rest only began first to be secured to him when the obligation of these Commandments came to be recognized.

The task of putting this Christian spirit into the old national customs was carried on also by a great Archbishop of Canterbury, Dunstan by name. Dunstan was more than an Archbishop; he was the Prime Minister of the time, and there is little doubt that the laws which bear the name of Edgar his King owe their origin to him.  These laws had to do with the better preservation of the peace, the pursuit of dishonest people, and the transaction of business in the presence of witnesses whose word could be trusted.  But Dunstan was Archbishop as well as Prime Minister, and as Archbishop he had to deal with a great matter which was agitating the English Church at the time, and we find him dealing with it in the broad spirit of a statesman rather than from the point of view of the narrow ecclesiastic. The standard of life within many of the monastic houses had for a long time been a cause for scandal; whilst the clergy who served the Cathedrals were men who, though belonging to a Common Chapter, lived as married men in their own houses, so that even where there was no cause for scandal it was said that the Church suffered because her ministers were occupied with worldly cares. Similar difficulties were being experienced abroad, and there they were being met by a new monastic rule far more severe than any which had hitherto been adopted. Bishop Ethelwold of Winchester, one of Dunstan's contemporaries, was eager that this new rule should be adopted in England and was ready to enforce its adoption at the point of the sword. Dunstan, however, tempered this indiscriminate zeal as far as he could, and in his own Chapter at Canterbury the Secular Canons, as they were called, lived on undisturbed so long as he was Archbishop.

Dunstan died in 988. Nearly eighty years after

—*i.e.*, in 1066—came the great Norman invasion. That invasion marks the beginning of a new period in English Church history. So far the English Church had lived on in a condition of complete independence of the rest of Christendom. The English Church was definitely national, and suffered the limitations while enjoying the freedom of such a position. It regarded itself as a part of a great whole, but it settled its own affairs without reference to outside authority. Once or twice indeed the Bishops of Rome had tried to take the position of an over-lord. On one occasion, in the eighth century, King Offa of Mercia had for his own ends welcomed the presence of a Papal Envoy. He wanted to create an Archbishopric at Lichfield, and so asked for outside aid against the protests of Canterbury. But the normal attitude of the English Church towards the Papacy was that of independence. Thus, when Bishop Wilfrid, one of the great Theodore's suffragans, had appealed to Rome against the action of the Archbishop in splitting up his diocese, he was put into prison by the King and Witan of Northumbria for so daring to take the case abroad. On another occasion Dunstan notwithstanding a Papal command refused to withdraw a sentence of excommunication which he had pronounced upon an English noble who was living in sin.

We see there was freedom from foreign control, but this freedom was not altogether for good. The English Church was living in a kind of backwater, scarcely at all sharing in the movement toward better things and toward the nobler civilization which was then affecting the Continent. Its life was becoming stagnant, and its influence for good daily less and less. It was at this time that the Normans came.

# CHAPTER II

THE Normans were men possessed of a vigour, spiritual and intellectual as well as physical, which was altogether new to English people. They were in the forefront of every movement on the Continent, and their coming to England meant great things for the English Church as well as for the English nation. Their methods were often rough and hard. They despised the English and were hated in return. But in numbers they were only as a handful in the measure. So they did not destroy the English, but came and lived amongst them, and acting like leaven infused a new life into every rank of society. The Church became strong again. Vigorous Norman Bishops first removed their sees from little country places to the great towns in their dioceses, and then began the building of their massive cathedral churches, and later on remodelled the services which were to be sung in them.

With this new life, however, came new problems. The Church in Normandy had been in close touch with Rome; its leaders shared with the great Hildebrand, the Pope of the time, in his reforming zeal. Should there then be any new relationship between the English Church and Rome? This important point was settled by the Conqueror himself. He said that no Pope should be recognized as Pope in England without the royal authority. He also defined the relation between the Church and the State by declaring that the Church should pass no new Canon or Church law without his consent, nor excommunicate any one of his servants without his consent. Both these rules were very important. The Canons of the Church at that time not only might deal with purely Church affairs, but might also treat of questions of marriage or of inheritances, and so might affect all classes of people. Excommunication also in those days carried with it serious civil consequences. A man under excommunication could no longer claim the allegiance of his retainers; by his excommunication he was also outlawed.

4

We recognize that the Conqueror meant his influence to be very real. Yet in another way he gave the Church greater liberty than it had ever had before. He separated the Church courts from the civil courts. Hitherto, cases dealing with every breach of Church law had come before the common court in which the Bishop had sat side by side with the Sheriff and the Alderman, and possessing only an authority equal with theirs had sometimes been obliged to allow Church cases to be lightly dealt with. But now William laid it down that the Bishops and Archdeacons should have their own courts where they could administer justice without let or hindrance, and he promised that if any of his subjects dared to show contempt for the authority of these new courts he would see that they were punished. Yet by thus setting up a separate set of courts within the kingdom the Conqueror did a thing which was destined, as we shall see, to be the cause of most serious trouble hereafter.

William was succeeded upon the throne by two sons in succession, and in the half-century during which they reigned two other great questions arose and received settlement.

One was called the Investiture Controversy.

Here the question at issue was whether lay persons should continue to invest bishops and others with the symbols of their office. The matter was one of the greatest importance; it involved the freedom of the Church. If laymen could really bestow ecclesiastical office then men of the character of the Rufus could foist whom they would into the highest positions of the Church and practically make the Church merely an instrument of their own tyranny. There would be small chance of men of the stamp of John the Baptist being made Bishops, while men like Herod might be Kings or great nobles. The question was settled by a compromise. On the occurrence of a vacancy in a bishopric or abbey, the Chapter were to choose someone in the King's presence, and the man thus chosen was to do homage to the King for the landed possessions of his new office, but he was to receive investiture at the hands of the Church. By this plan the King got all he could rightly claim—viz., the allegiance of the ecclesiastics in his kingdom, and inasmuch as the election was to take place in his presence he could usually secure the election of his nominee. But he gave up his claim to appoint whom he would and to give them himself the symbols of their office.

The other question was originally purely a national one and seemed at times, indeed, to be only a rather petty quarrel between two ecclesiastics; but it was settled in a way that brought infinite trouble upon the English Church. For many years the Archbishop of Canterbury had been trying to secure from the Archbishop of York an acknowledgment of his precedence, and the case had been referred to Rome for decision. The Pope of Rome at the time saw in this question an opportunity for making more real the power of the Roman See over the English Church. The great method by which the Popes made their influence felt in different countries was by the sending of Legates who, invested with Papal authority, were able to bring to bear at any given place and upon any given cause the whole weight of Papal authority. Until well on in the twelfth century the attempts of the Popes to send Legates to England had always been stoutly resisted; but in 1123 the King, Henry I., and the Archbishop of Canterbury alike were false to the real interests of the English Church. The Archbishop had again complained to Rome of the contumacy of the Archbishop of York, and the Pope had promised that the case should be decided in England at a

Council over which a Papal Legate should preside.
The Legate came, and he was welcomed not only
by the Archbishop but also by the King. For
the King having lost his only son at sea was
endeavouring to secure for his daughter Matilda the
succession to the crown, and so received the Legate
in the hope that he might thus get the support of
the Papal influence in his schemes for his daughter.
The Papal Legate did many things, but he did not
settle the vexed question of the relative positions
of Canterbury and York, and the matter was again
referred to Rome, and finally, in 1126, was decided
in a fashion which while it bore unmistakable witness to the astuteness of Rome bore equal witness
to the folly of the Archbishop. The Pope told the
Archbishop that there was a way out of the difficulty which would settle the question for ever in
favour of Canterbury, and that was that in future
the Archbishop should always be the Legate of
Rome in England. The Archbishop accepted this,
and by doing so gained his point with regard to
York but bartered away the freedom of the English
Church. We must not make too much, however,
of the cunning of the Pope or of the folly of the
Archbishop. Both were influenced to a degree
which it is difficult for us in these days to gauge by

the so-called Decretals of Isidore. These Decretals
professed to be a collection of Papal decisions of
the first and second centuries, and had been put
forward during the ninth century by some unknown Continental writer. Some of them were
altogether false; others were given a false importance because they were said to belong to a far
earlier time than was really the case. But the
world accepted them all as genuine, and since they
all asserted in one way or another the sovereignty
of the Papacy over the whole of Christendom it
followed naturally that there could be no longer
any place within the universal Church for independent National Churches. To disobey a Pope or to
refuse to recognize his Legate seemed to be equiva-
lent to opposing the revealed will of Heaven. It
was these decrees which made the medieval Papacy.
They were quoted by every Pope in succession as
he strove to extend the authority of his see, and it
was the belief in their genuineness which made it
always difficult for the English Church to assert its
independence of Rome. With these documents in
his hands a Pope could boldly claim to settle questions dealing either with precedence or with any
other matter, and an Archbishop, having read them,
might feel that to act as Papal Legate was the

highest office to which he could aspire. Nevertheless the result was disastrous. Whatever authority
the head of the English Church might in future
exercise in England, it would always be possible for
the Popes to say that that authority was derived
from them and did not belong of itself to the archbishopric.

The two sons of the great Conqueror were succeeded by their nephew, Stephen of Blois. His
reign is spoken of by the chronicler of the time as
a ' dreary nineteen winters.' It was a time of
terrible anarchy, every man doing that which was
right in his own eyes. The machinery of civil
administration went to pieces entirely and the
Church courts were the only courts left in which
people could seek for justice. Hence of course
these Church courts widened the area of their
jurisdiction, and the people were glad that they
did so. It was better to have Church courts than
none at all.

But when in 1154 Stephen died and Henry II.
was crowned King, the whole aspect of affairs
was changed. This Henry was the greatest
man of his time, and he came to the throne of
England with a resolute determination to put an
end to the disorder which existed throughout the

land. With his coming the foreign hired soldiery
disappeared like the morning mist; the strong
castles of the nobles, which had been erected without royal permission and which formed a constant
menace to the poor folk near them, were destroyed;
evil-doers of every sort found little mercy. The new
King had also to reconstruct the civil machinery
which had been begun by his grandfather, Henry I.
But so soon as he attempted to do this the whole
question of the jurisdiction of the Church courts
came into prominence. Two things were clear to
the King's mind. One was that these Church
courts existing within his own kingdom and dealing with his own subjects were acting in entire
independence of his authority, and giving decisions
based on a code of law which was not royal
law; the other was that these same decisions
seemed oftentimes to be scandalously lacking in
severity. On both points the King was right, but
it was with regard to the second that the nation
felt most keenly. The practice of the Church
courts was that if a man accused before them and
found guilty of an offence could prove that he
held "Orders" in the Church, then he was
"unfrocked" for the offence—that is, deprived of
his Orders. But we need to remember that in those

days there were seven Orders in the Church—
namely, priests (including Bishops), deacons, sub-
deacons, acolytes, exorcists, lectors (readers), and
ostiarii (doorkeepers), and that since the fact of
being in minor Orders did not in the least degree
interfere with a man's ordinary calling in life a
large proportion of the male population were in one
or other of the minor Orders.   Many people indeed
sought for these minor Orders knowing that in
this way they could claim the protection of the
Church courts, and if accused of a crime would be
tried by the same courts, and if convicted only
unfrocked.   Thus, two men in the same neighbourhood might be equally guilty of murder, but if one
had chanced to have obtained minor Orders at
some earlier date, he for his offence would simply
receive a sentence from the Church courts for
which he would care very little, while the other
would have to face the severity of the civil court.

Such a condition of things was intolerable.
Therefore, when in 1162 there was a vacancy in
the Archbishopric of Canterbury, Henry seized the
opportunity to secure an Archbishop who, he
hoped, would help him to put matters on a right
footing.   The King's intimate friend and Minister,
Thomas Becket, became the new Archbishop.   But

Henry found at once that instead of providing for himself an assistant he had given to the Church courts a champion possessed of a will as strong and as inflexible as his own. Misunderstandings on various points arose and had created a breach between the King and the Archbishop long before the King brought forward the celebrated Constitutions of Clarendon ; so that when the great question as to the jurisdiction of the Church courts came to be debated there existed a feeling of mutual suspicion and hostility which made it impossible for either man to see fairly the aims of the other. The King's new suggestion was that if a man holding any Orders within the Church was accused of crime he should be tried as heretofore by the Church courts, and if found to be guilty should be unfrocked by those courts ; but that also, in future, a royal officer should be waiting at the door of the Church court to arrest the man—now, of course, a layman because unfrocked—and carry him off to receive in addition the punishment due to the offence from the civil court.

As we look back we can see that the King's proposal was an eminently wise one. The Archbishop, however, and many others were filled with alarm. They dreaded this measure as being probably only the first of many attempts to limit the authority of the Church. They feared any increase of lay jurisdiction, and when we remember that the terrible days of Stephen had scarcely yet come to an end, and that the unrighteous rule of the Rufus was still a bitter memory, we can understand why it seemed to the Archbishop and his friends that they had good cause for being anxious. If there had been any friendliness between Henry and Thomas there is no doubt that an agreement could have been found without much difficulty. Both men were possessed of real greatness of character and both desired the common good. But it was just that friendliness which was so conspicuously absent. The King thereupon tried to coerce the Archbishop, and the Archbishop fearing for his life fled to France. Then followed six unhappy years of mutual recrimination, during which time the Archbishop remained in exile. In 1170, however, the quarrel was patched up, and the Archbishop returned to Canterbury. But he returned apparently only to be murdered. On the evening of December 29 of that year four knights, using some hasty words of the King as a cloak for their own evil desires, made an attack upon the Archbishop within the precincts of his own cathedral and finally slew him. Such a deed proved the greatest possible hindrance in the way of Henry's reforms. Nothing else, indeed, was attempted with regard to the Church, for the people looked upon Thomas as a martyr. Consequently, the whole question of the rightful jurisdiction of the Church courts was left unsettled, and remained unsettled for several generations, and there was continual bickering between the civil judges who administered the King's law, and the ecclesiastical judges who administered Church law.

But there were also other people in the time of Henry II. who feared the effect of his other reforms. The problem that Henry had to face was how to make the central authority—*i.e.*, the King's authority—so strong that peace and good order might be secured for rich and poor alike throughout the country. It was to this end that he directed all his legislation. But it is clear that a central authority if it were strong might prove to be a tyranny in the hands of an unrighteous man, producing hardships greater even than those which arise when there is an absence of a central authority altogether. This did actually happen in the reign of Henry's son, John, and it was with the object of securing definite limits to this uncontrolled tyranny that Archbishop Stephen Langton and the

nobles of John's time compelled him to sign the
Great Charter. This event in English history is
one of those that are best known by people generally, but the part played by Stephen Langton is
worthy of being mentioned again. It was he who not
only gave the Barons something definite to strive for
by recalling to them the Charter of Liberties issued
by John's great grandfather, Henry I., but who was
also the constant means of keeping them together
and inspiring their action. John himself realized
that the main strength of the opposition came from
the Church, and he tried to quiet the Church by
making promises to the Bishops that he would grant
them what they wanted. The Bishops, however,
kept loyally to their friends and refused to be dealt
with separately. In yet another way also the
great Archbishop made his influence felt. One of
the characteristics of the Great Charter is its
attempt to secure privileges for all classes in the
kingdom—*i.e.*, for the small farmer who only had
his few agricultural implements, and for the
merchant who only had his merchandise, as much
as for the great baron and the great ecclesiastic.
This attempt was due to the great Archbishop, and
how really and truly it was his work was seen
when on the Charter being re-issued in 1216

and again in 1217 (the years in which the Archbishop was in disgrace at Rome), many of the clauses dealing with the rights of the mass of the people were either omitted altogether or seriously modified.

This time of struggle for political freedom had other and less happy consequences for the nation from a Church point of view. To understand this we need to go back somewhat. Nine years before the signing of the Great Charter Langton had been made Archbishop of Canterbury. King John, however, had wished that a certain John de Grey, Bishop of Norwich, should be made Archbishop, and when he heard that Langton had been elected, through the intervention of the Pope, he was furious. The Pope of the time, however, was a man who did not regard with much concern the fury of Kings. This Pope, Innocent III. by name, takes rank with the greatest of the occupants of the Papal Chair. He combined a wonderful patience in working and an untiring watchfulness for opportunities with a striking boldness of action when he felt that action was required. In recommending the monks of Canterbury to elect Stephen Langton to the archbishopric he acted solely from the highest motives, and when he found that King

John refused to receive him as Archbishop, he proceeded to force the King into submission. He began by placing England under an interdict. This sentence, however, did not affect John very much. It made his people suffer indeed, for they were deprived of all the public services of the Church except those required by extreme necessity. But his people's troubles were no trouble to John. In the year following the King was excommunicated, but neither did that affect him. Then two years later Innocent threatened to depose him and to use Philip Augustus, the powerful French King, to make the sentence of deposition effective. At last the King gave way, frightened, it is said, by the prophecies which had been spoken concerning him more than by the prospect of a French invasion. But whatever the cause which led the King to make his submission, there is no doubt about the abject nature of it. Near Dover he met two envoys from the Pope, and to them, as representing the Pope, he surrendered his kingdom, and consented to receive it back as a tenant received land from an overlord. The Pope now regarded himself as the owner of England and the protector of John, and the King hoped that in this way he would save himself from the opposition of the

Barons as well as from an invasion from France.
In neither case were his hopes fully realized,
though the support of the Papacy proved very
valuable to him.  For a short while all went well
for him, but in 1214 his forces in alliance with
those of Flanders and the Empire were routed
at Bouvines in Flanders by Philip of France.
This so weakened John's power that he no longer
dared resist the Barons, but signed the Great
Charter in the following year.  But no sooner
had he done so than he appealed to Pandolf,
who was now Papal Legate and as such the
representative of the King's overlord, and asked
him for his protection.  Pandolf, taking the view
that the Papal influence would be increased if
the Pope supported the King, sent a garbled
account of the recent events in England to his
master in Rome, and Innocent, relying on the
information sent to him, annulled the Charter,
excommunicated John's enemies, and suspended
Langton from his office as Archbishop.  The Barons
thereupon took matters into their own hands,
and offered the crown of England to Louis, the
son of the King of France.  This they did in the
autumn of 1215.  Before the end of the year
French troops had begun to arrive, and Louis him-

self came in the following May. The beginning of
a bitter struggle seemed in sight, but in October,
1216, John died at Newark, and at once the whole
complexion of affairs was altered. The English
Barons who had been supporting Louis did not in
reality desire a French King to reign over them;
they had only regarded such an event as less intolerable than the continued reign of John. Now
that John was dead a large number of them readily
jumped at any excuse by which they could justify
their desertion of the Prince whom they themselves had invited to England. In these difficult
circumstances the Papacy played an exceedingly
important part. Gualo had succeeded Pandolf as
Papal Legate. There was a new Pope indeed at
Rome, for Innocent had died and had been succeeded by Honorius III.; but though there was a
new Pope there was no new policy, and Gualo,
realizing this, acted with great resolution on behalf
of John's son, Prince Henry, a lad nine years of
age. There is no doubt that the action of the
Legate saved England from civil strife. The
coronation of the boy-King was secured and many
of the Barons were won over.

The story of this troubled time needs thus to be
told with some detail if we would understand the

history of the following fifty-six years during which
period this Henry was King. Throughout this
long half-century it is hardly surprising that Henry
never once offered any opposition to the Papal
encroachments. He owed his crown to Papal
action; he was reared under Papal influence. He
never realized what he might have gained by
resistance. Resistance, indeed, seemed an impossibility, for the whole world of the time was wit-
nessing the humiliation at the hands of the Pope
of Henry's brother-in-law, the great Frederick II.
of Germany. For the first twelve years of his
reign Stephen Langton lived on, and for the last
twenty-five years an uncle by marriage, a foreigner,
Boniface of Savoy, held the archbishopric, and
either the Englishman or the foreigner would have
taken part gladly in a policy of opposition to
Rome if only the King had given them a lead;
but nothing was farther from his thoughts.

# CHAPTER III

ALTHOUGH the country complained bitterly of the
way in which it was drained of money to fill
the Papal coffers, it was forced to confess that
it owed much to the wonderful work done in the
name of religion in the early years of the thirteenth
century by the Mendicant Orders—Orders which
existed by Papal authority and which were aided
by Papal help. The first of these Orders, the
Dominicans, took their name from Dominic of
Spain and, like their founder, laboured to
suppress the heresies prevalent at the time.
The Franciscans, the followers of Francis of
Assisi, began with the idea of simply living a life
as nearly Christlike as possible in the midst of a
naughty world ; they renounced all property and
spent their time in doing good works. The two
Orders came to be known in England as the
" Black Friars " and " Grey Friars," for the

43

Dominicans wore a black habit and the Franciscans a grey.  Though originally quite distinct yet they came into prominence almost at the same time, and before long each borrowed the characteristic mark of the other.  The Dominicans adopted the rule of voluntary poverty from the Franciscans, and the Franciscans became diligent students of theology.  The effect of this combined movement upon the life of the time was so great that it may be said to have changed the face of Europe.  A new spirit seemed to be at work in society ; once more life was believed to be worth living ; once again men realized that it was possible to be happy apart from material possessions.  Both Orders, however, owed much of their success to the fact that from the first they were recognized by the Pope, and thus it came about that they were loyal supporters of the Papacy.  As they grew they came to include within their ranks men out of every nation in Europe ; but it made little difference from whence they gathered their members, since almost every member lost all national feeling in an enthusiasm for Rome.  The two Orders became, in fact, a kind of irregular army waging a constant warfare on behalf of Rome against the claims of independent national Churches.  Their influence in this direction, however, was only recognized at a later date. In the early years of the thirteenth century they were welcomed in all places without reserve. If other countries owed them much, England owed them more. Within forty years they had revolutionized the land. In an age of oligarchical tyranny they protected the weak; in an age of darkness they taught the ignorant; in an age of much moral corruption they lived lives of holiness. They appealed to the common people in a way that the monastic orders had never done. The monk lived in his monastery in order to escape the corruption of the world, and so to win a way for himself into Paradise. The friar lived in the world in order, if possible, to lessen its corruption, and so to help *others* to win a way into Paradise. It is not to be wondered at that the friars made religion popular as it had never been before. It is equally easy to understand that while such men were at work in the world it would be difficult to struggle with the Papacy which they reverenced and obeyed. Nevertheless, people in high position did realize that the Papacy was coming to stand more and more for extortion and corruption. One of the thirteenth-century Bishops, Robert Grosseteste, won for himself undying fame by reason of his persistent opposition to Rome. He was, indeed, on one occasion temporarily suspended from his office because he would not admit an Italian to a rich benefice on account of his ignorance of English. Yet this same Grosseteste was an enthusiastic supporter of the Mendicants. He had been the first Rector of the Franciscans at Oxford, and he supported them to the day of his death.

The influence of the Mendicants as political agents of the Papacy only began to be felt in the reign of Edward I. Edward I. succeeded his father, Henry III., in 1272. He was anxious to complete the work that had been begun so splendidly by Henry II. He wished amongst other things to define as clearly as possible the relative powers of Church and State, and the better to secure this end he endeavoured on two occasions to get the Archbishopric for his Chancellor, Robert Burnell. But the Papacy of Edward's time was a very different thing from the Papacy of Henry's time. On each occasion not only did the Papacy put on one side the royal nomination, but also on each occasion disregarded the choice of the monks of Canterbury in whom was vested by canonical right the power of election, and on the first occasion

Kilwardby, a Dominican friar, and on the second
John Peckham, a Franciscan, was forced upon
the English Church. The motive for this action
on the part of the Papacy is clear. It was felt
that the Archbishop should be in future some-
body who would uphold the Papal pretensions.
Kilwardby disappointed the Pope from this point
of view, and he was therefore made a Cardinal so
that, inasmuch as Cardinals had to live in Rome,
he should resign the Archbishopric. Peckham
was a man of very different stamp. No one
doubted for a moment his honesty and his selfless-
ness, but he was a rigid supporter of the Papacy
and possessed little of the tact needed in a successful statesman. No sooner had he arrived in England
than he made it quite clear what his attitude
would be. He pronounced against the holding
of benefices in plurality ; he ordered the clergy to
put up in their churches a copy of the Great
Charter and told them to declare to their people
that those who broke the terms of the Charter
were, by such conduct, excommunicate ; and, further,
he proceeded in the exercise of his archiepiscopal
power to inquire in no sparing fashion into the
conduct of the Bishops of his province. In such
ways he stirred up opposition to himself in every

quarter; but the person who was most indignant
was the King, who saw in the action of the
Archbishop with regard to the observance of the
Great Charter a reflection on the royal conduct,
and he was not slow to retaliate.

In 1279, a few weeks after Peckham's ill-judged
proceedings, Edward secured the passing of the
Statute of Mortmain which declared that in future
no grants of land should be made to the Church
without the permission of the overlord of the
person making the grant.  If the permission was
not first sought for then the land became forfeit to
the overlord.   There is  no  question that  the
Statute was a shrewd blow directed against the
Church, but it had its origin not merely in Edward's
resentment at the action of his new Archbishop,
but also in the very general feeling at the time that
some such check was really needful for the well-
being of the State, since it was notorious that
many of the grants of land which had been made
to the Church were made merely in a fraudulent
spirit.  A man who held land from an overlord was
bound by the conditions of feudal tenure to render
certain services to his overlord, and the overlord
had in addition certain privileges with regard to
that land which at any moment might become a

source of profit to him. Thus, for instance, he had the wardship of the land if the heir of his tenant was under age when the tenant died; he had the right of bestowing the hand of heiresses in marriage; and, moreover, if there were a failure of heirs, the land escheated to him as overlord. But the moment land came into the possession of an abbey or priory the interests of the overlord were seriously endangered. It was far less easy to compel an abbey to fulfil the services due than it was to compel an individual. Moreover, abbeys and priories never died and so there was no question in their case of profits being made made out of wardship, or of heiresses being bestowed in marriage, or of land escheating to the overlord. It was under these circumstances that the Statute was so welcomed by the great lords. The principle of it, indeed, has remained a part of the law of England until this day, since a special procedure has to be followed before land can be given for ecclesiastical purposes, even for the building of a suburban church.

The quarrel between King and Archbishop did not end there. Peckham stirred up again the question of the rival jurisdiction of the King's courts and the Church courts, and here also the result was in the main a victory for the King, for in 1285 Edward issued a writ called *Circumspecte Agatis* in which the extent of the ecclesiastical jurisdiction was defined as clearly and as narrowly as possible. It was admitted that the Church courts had jurisdiction in matrimonial and testamentary cases, and could deal with offences for which penance was due and with all questions relating to tithes, mortuaries, churches and churchyards, perjury and defamation ; but yet the writ meant practically a defeat for the Church, for its very definiteness made it impossible for the Church in the future to attempt to draw into its courts any cases other than those named.

Seven years later Archbishop Peckham died. 'Humble brother John,' as he was called by the Franciscans, had all along kept the regard of his King although King and Archbishop had differed so widely in opinion. The vacancy was on this occasion canonically filled up, not indeed because neither the Papacy nor the King had a desire any longer to override the rights of diocesan chapters, but because it happened that at the moment the Papacy was vacant and the King had neither a favourite Chancellor nor other official for whom he was eager to get the Archbishopric. The choice of the chapter fell upon Robert of Winchelsea; and it was significant that Winchelsea was neither a Dominican nor a Franciscan nor even a member of a monastic body. He was none the less, however, a man well fitted for the post. It is even said that he was so well thought of at Rome, where he had to wait twelve months for the confirmation of his election, that it was supposed that he might himself be elected Pope.

The new Archbishop found before long that he had an exceedingly difficult part to play. The Pope who confirmed his election had been compelled to resign and was afterwards shut up in a pestilential castle, and died there. The new Pope was Boniface VIII., the man who was commonly suspected of being responsible for the death of his predecessor. This Boniface was a clever pretentious man, and eager to play the part of a great ecclesiastical statesman. He fancied he could be another Hildebrand or Innocent III. He did not see that the times had completely altered. Edward I. of England was now quarrelling with Philip IV. of France, and Boniface peremptorily ordered them to put up their swords and accept his mediation. This both the Kings refused to do, whereupon the Pope endeavoured to compel them to obedience by issuing the celebrated Bull *Clericis Laicos* in which the clergy of the two kingdoms were ordered not to pay any taxes to the secular power without the permission of the Papacy. The Bull placed Winchelsea and the clergy of England in a great difficulty. Edward was insistent in his demands for money. What was to be done? In January, 1297, the Archbishop preaching at St. Paul's said that the clergy had two lords to obey, the King and the Pope, and if the question ever arose as to which they should obey, there could be no doubt that they must obey the Pope rather than the King. The King was exceedingly angry and proceeded to declare the clergy outlawed, and tried by acts of bitter and sometimes rather petty hostility to dragoon the Archbishop into submission. Winchelsea, however, remained immovable, and both he and the clergy received much sympathy from the laity, not indeed because the laity were pleased that the clergy should hold by the Pope rather than by the King, but because the laity themselves were smarting under the burden of taxation which had become necessary by reason of Edward's foreign policy. Discontent, in fact, was growing on all sides, and came to a head during Edward's absence in Flanders. The Archbishop and the leaders of the Barons compelled the Regency to reissue the Great Charter with the addition of certain new clauses which forebade the collection of taxes without the consent of Parliament, and Edward was in such a position that he had to accept this significant development in constitutional principle.

This *Confirmatio Cartarum*, as it is called, is one of the great landmarks in English history. Edward himself had brought Parliament in its modern sense into existence. He was the first King to summon a complete representation of the different estates of the realm to meet and consult on public affairs. Now by giving up to it this control over taxation he gave it its greatest power. Throughout the troubled years which preceded this concession on the part of the King it was the clergy, and especially the Archbishop, whose example put heart into the resistance against the King's arbitrary taxation. Edward saw this clearly enough, and he came back from Flanders filled with indignation against the Archbishop. Winchelsea, however, for the time was regarded as having championed the national cause and so occupied far too strong a position for the King to harm him.

Edward meanwhile nursed his anger, until at last came his opportunity for revenge. Boniface

died in 1308, and in 1305 Philip IV. of France
secured the election of Bertrand de Goth, Archbishop of Bordeaux, who took the title of Clement V.
The new Pope, who had been one of Edward's
subjects in Gascony, seemed almost as anxious
to please Edward as Philip.   He absolved the
English King from his oath with regard to the
Forest Laws, and added that the King in future
was never to be excommunicated without Papal
permission.   But most significant of all, he listened
to Edward's complaints against the Archbishop of
Canterbury and summoned the latter to appear before the Papal Court.   When Winchelsea thereupon
presented himself to Edward to obtain his formal
permission to leave the country, Edward made it
clear how deeply he hated the Archbishop and how
he rejoiced at being rid of him.   ' We gladly give
you permission to go,' he said, ' but we will never
give you permission to return.'   Here, again, it is
evident how difficult a part the English Church
had to play.   It formed part of the Catholic Church
and acknowledged, as all men did then, that the
Pope was God's ruler of the Church on earth, yet
it could never really depend upon the support of
the Popes if political considerations tempted them
to desert it.   Clement V. acted simply at the wish

of a revengeful King, and Winchelsea suffered
because he had striven to be faithful to the Papacy.

But the Pontificate of Clement V. is chiefly remembered for the fact that with him began what is
known as the ' Babylonish Captivity.' The discord
of parties in Rome, and indeed throughout Italy,
disturbed Clement so greatly that he took up his
residence at Avignon, a town situated in what is now
South-Eastern France but which was in Clement's
time a part of the possessions of Charles II. of Naples,
who was also Count of Provence ; but the town was
so near to the dominions of the French King that
the Pope fell naturally and immediately under his
influence. This residence at Avignon was destined
to have most serious consequences for the Papacy,
for so long as the Popes remained there it was
difficult for them to convince the world that they
were independent. To English people especially it
seemed that they were becoming little else than
tools in the hands of the French King. To the old
hatred of the Papacy as an extortionate pleader for
money was now added a new hatred because it was
believed to be using its spiritual authority to
advance the interests of England's enemy. This
new dislike found expression in one of the last
Statutes of Edward's reign—namely, the famous

Statute of Carlisle passed in 1307.  By this Statute
an endeavour was made to put a stop to the sending of money out of the kingdom by monks or their
agents.  It is the first of the many anti-Papal
Statutes which have been passed by English Parliaments.  In the discussion which preceded its passing many other grievances were brought forward,
such as the abuses of Papal patronage, the promotion of aliens, the reservation of first-fruits, and
other exactions.  In a word, now that there was a
national Parliament in existence national feeling
began to express itself unmistakeably ; and the more
it came to be seen that the Pope had become little
else than a French political agent the feeling of the
nation against his interference in English Church
affairs grew apace.  ' Lord Jesus,' cried a writer of
the times, ' remove the Pope from off our backs or
curb his power.'

Yet the Kings when it suited their purpose were
as glad as ever to make use of their influence.  Thus
when Winchelsea was removed, a certain Walter
Reynolds, a royal nominee, was put by Pope
Clement into the vacancy in spite of the fact that
another man had been elected by the Chapter.  As
a matter of fact, by this time the diocesan Chapters
had lost almost entirely all control over the filling

up of vacant bishoprics. Hence we read of Bishops who were quite unworthy of the position they held but who had obtained advancement by bribery or influence, and it soon followed that the national Church sank lower and lower in the estimation of the people, since ignorant and slothful Bishops meant non-resident priests and neglected parishes. The old monastic houses, moreover, seemed now to be merely homes for men who tried to escape from bearing a share of the public burdens. The common people did not always distinguish between the good and the bad. Bishop Stapledon of Exeter was put to death by a London mob with a butcher's knife, and the Bishop of Rochester of the time had to fortify his manor-houses that he might live in comparative safety. There were signs of a growing discontent everywhere.

All other national troubles, however, sank for the moment into comparative unimportance beside that produced by the terrible pestilence which broke out in the middle of the fourteenth century. This pestilence, which has of late come to be called the 'Black Death,' was brought to England by the sailors of a ship which had been trading at Genoa where the plague was already in existence. Once in England it spread with terrible rapidity. Two

hundred people died daily in London when it was
at its height, whilst so terrible was the scourge in
the city of Norwich that two people died out of
every three, and Norwich, from being the second
city in the kingdom, was reduced to being the
sixth.   In the East Anglian diocese 863 fresh
institutions to benefices took place at this time, and
other parts of England could tell a similar tale.

The effect in every department of life of a plague
so general and so fatal was of course tremendous.
The Church was influenced by it as well as the
State, for among the victims were many of the
best of the clergy, and for want of fit men to fill
the numerous vacancies others altogether inefficient
were oftentimes appointed.

The pestilence, however, produced an even more
serious result than this.   By reason of the many
deaths agricultural labourers became scarce, and
those that remained demanded higher wages for
their services.  They cannot be blamed for this, for the
price of food had risen enormously ; yet the people
who employed labourers, including as a rule the
clergy, tried to compel the labourers to work at the
old rate of wages ; the clergy, that is, were throw-
ing in their lot with the rich as against the poor.
For the first time in English history the National

Church was taking up a Tory position. It had grown strong originally because it had won the love of the people and in a peculiar degree it could claim to be a National Church. But in the half-century preceding the outbreak of the pestilence it had been losing its hold, and now it quickly forfeited almost all of what remained to it of the popular regard.

As the fourteenth century drew to an end the condition of the country only became worse. Amongst the poorer classes there was much grievous suffering, and out of this sprang a bitterness of discontent which finally brought about the Peasant Revolt of 1381. Amongst the wealthier classes there was a common absence of the sense of responsibility coupled with much wanton and ostentatious extravagance. It was in the dark days of the pestilence that Edward III. founded with great display and expense the Order of the Garter, a new order which was supposed to be a new order of chivalry, but in which there was no real pursuit of noble ideals. Noble ideals seemed to be, indeed, forgotten. During the whole of this time scarcely any great Churchman came to the front. The sadness of the age is seen in Langland's celebrated poem of ' The Vision of William concerning Piers the Ploughman,' which complains bitterly of abuses and corruptions everywhere ; the parish priests were no true pastors ; the friars were wandering rogues ; the law courts were debased by bribery and extortion ; the craftsmen were idle and dissolute ; and impudent beggars infested the highways. Yet to Langland the reform required was not a reform in the social order or in the religious teaching of the time, but rather a reform in the lives of men themselves. In this way he forms a striking contrast to his contemporary John Wycliffe.

# CHAPTER IV

## WYCLIFFE

WYCLIFFE is the most striking figure in the English life of the latter part of the fourteenth century. Sprung from sturdy Yorkshire stock, he was sent to Oxford and won there great reputation, partly by reason of his extensive learning (he was probably the greatest scholar of his day), but more by reason of his personal character. He was exceeding thorough in all that he did and he was transparently honest. In addition, he possessed in a wonderful degree the power of imparting his knowledge to others and of converting his hearers into enthusiastic disciples. He first became popular in the political world in connection with the question as to whether the payment of the tribute which John had promised to the Papacy should be continued. It was Wycliffe who drew up the statement upon which it was finally decided that the payment should cease. His position was that the

Pope could not rightly claim the tribute inasmuch as neither Christ nor His Apostles had held property, and even if the tribute could be claimed by the Pope, then certainly in return the Pope ought to do his best for the good of the country from which the tribute came, instead of, as was really the case, constantly supporting that country's enemies. Further, he said that people living in sin had no right to authority or property of any kind. These arguments Wycliffe afterwards worked up into formal treatises, and it became clear to all men that to Wycliffe's mind the Church ought not to hold property at all; and when Wycliffe was told that the Church might proceed to excommunicate people who accepted such views, his reply was that excommunication need only be dreaded by men who were living in sin, and that the position of a righteous man towards God was not affected by any sentence passed upon him by the Church.

This teaching with regard to Church endowments was greedily laid hold of by a large party in the State who, under the leadership of the unscrupulous John of Gaunt the third son of Edward III., were eager to enrich themselves at the expense of the Church. The Church for its part was not slow to resist this attack upon its wealth, and Wycliffe was accordingly summoned to appear before the Bishops in S. Paul's Cathedral in 1377. Nothing, however, came of this attempt to suppress Wycliffe, for the whole proceedings abruptly terminated in a scuffle which took place in the cathedral itself—a scuffle which arose out of the indignation of the Londoners who were present at the insulting attitude adopted by John of Gaunt towards their Bishop. In the confusion Wycliffe was taken from the cathedral and the matter was allowed to drop for the time.

In the following year an event occurred which probably did more than all else to convert Wycliffe into a bitter opponent of the whole Papal position. In 1377 the 'Babylonish Captivity' had come to an end, and the Popes who had lived at Avignon for seventy years returned once again to Rome. In 1378, however, on the occurrence of a vacancy in the Papal Chair, two Popes were elected, and one of them, the nominee of the French Cardinals, went back to Avignon. Christendom now witnessed the shocking spectacle of rival Popes hurling bitter anathemas one against the other. But while other good men grieved sorely over this distressing state of things Wycliffe was stirred into questioning the very position of the Papacy itself—that is, for

him the question was not which of the two Popes
had most right on his side, but whether the office
which each claimed was one in accordance with the
will of God. From this time also he appealed
no longer merely to scholars but to the people.
Hitherto he had written elaborate works in Latin;
now he began to write tracts in English. Moreover, so that his doctrines might be carried far and
wide he organized a system of itinerant 'poor
priests,' and into the hands of these agents of his he
before long put an instrument far more valuable
even than his tracts—namely, the Bible in English.

So long as Wycliffe and his disciples taught
simply the necessity for a greater personal holiness
and only made attacks upon the Papal position,
they were, on the whole, generally popular; but
when Wycliffe began to attack the doctrine of
Transubstantiation by saying that whilst there was
a Real Presence of Christ in the Eucharist there was
no change in the substance of the bread and wine,
he was met at once by a storm of opposition.
Even John of Gaunt deserted him. Still, it is
doubtful how far he would have lost his popularity
had it not been that in 1381 there occurred the
rising of the peasants in Kent and in the Eastern
Counties. Some of Wycliffe's 'poor priests' were

certainly connected with this movement, and it became a common charge against him and his followers that they were altogether responsible for it. The rising seemed to be for a time exceedingly serious, and the violence of it is seen in the murder of Simon of Sudbury, the Archbishop of Canterbury of the time.

The effect of it, however, was to unite all the various conservative elements in the country. Those who dreaded changes in the Church joined hands with those who feared social disorganization. Religious questions and economic questions became inextricably mixed up, and a condition of things in ecclesiastical affairs out of which the English Church might have come freed from the thraldom of Rome, ultimately produced no good result whatever. How strong was the desire to assert the independence of the National Church is to be seen in the Statute of Provisors of 1390, which reinforced the earlier Statutes of 1351 and 1362, and in the great Statute of Præmunire of 1393, which forbade in the strongest terms the carrying of appeals to Rome. But this legislation was never really effective, for those who supported it most enthusiastically were just those who came to be regarded more and more as political agitators. These people—Lollards as they were called—half religious, half socialistic in their aims, roused the fears of the country nobility and gentry quite as much as the dislike of the Church. They seemed to be aiming at the destruction of the whole social fabric as it then existed, and it was to deal with them that the terrible Statutes for the burning of heretics were passed. The suggestion to make use of burning as a means of stamping out agitators came first of all from the Church, but it was readily adopted by Parliament, for Parliament was an assembly representing the landholding interest. The eagerness of the laity to suppress these disturbers is seen more definitely still in the Statute of 1414, by which the slackness of the Church in laying hands upon them was remedied by giving power also to the sheriffs to arrest for heresy.

Persecution which was thus approved of both by the Church and the State killed before long all attempts at reform of every sort. The teaching of Wycliffe became forgotten in England. It lived on, however, in Bohemia whither it had been carried by Bohemian students who had been taught by Wycliffe at Oxford, and in Bohemia it found expression in the doctrines of Huss and in this way later on it gave direction to the thoughts of

Luther. But in England for a time every other question was forgotten in the presence of the glamour created by the great military successes of Henry V. over France, the old national enemy ; whilst after the death of Henry V. battles, first abroad and then at home, engrossed the nation for nearly three-quarters of a century more.

But in spite of social disturbance and the turmoil of war, a work which was to prove of the greatest help in the national life had its origin in this time. William of Wykeham, Bishop of Winchester from 1367 to 1404, built not only his New College at Oxford, but also that school at Winchester which has served as a model for all the famous public schools of the country. It was in imitation of the good Bishop's work that half a century later Henry VI. founded the school at Eton and his King's College at Cambridge. The aim of Bishop and King was one and the same— namely, that by a true education the youth of the land might be the better trained to serve God both in Church and State.

# CHAPTER V

FROM the middle of the fifteenth century onwards
for 200 years Europe generally, as well as
England in particular, was agitated to a degree
unknown before over questions of religion, and
when it is remembered that those questions dealt
with the very essentials of the Faith no one can
wonder at the disturbance they produced. The
general title for the period is that of the Reformation, but such a title is not an altogether satisfactory one, for it implies only that something
was done that needed the doing ; that errors were
exploded and abuses rectified ; and it does not
even suggest that there was with the reform any
accompaniment of evil. And yet most assuredly
with the good that was done was mixed up much
that was bad. Not only was there great destruction
of things that were beautiful and of priceless worth ;
not only were methods which had proved helpful

in the past rudely and thoughtlessly cast on one side as being altogether useless—such mistakes could have been remedied with comparative ease ; but the movement produced also a fearful development of partisan spirit, with the result that large bodies of Christians lost all continuity with the Church of Christ, while the Church itself became torn and rent asunder.  Some of the great actors of the time were ignorantly zealous, some were timid and vacillating, some were among the most unscrupulous and worthless men that have ever wielded the power of authority and whose imperfections were as fruitful for mischief as the splendid work done by the best men was productive of good.  Something of all this will be learnt hereafter, but  the mention of it here will enable us to use the title of the Reformation as the common title of the period without being blind to the fact that the Church came out of the crisis in many respects maimed, and in many respects weakened in its effectiveness as a witness for righteousness against the powers of evil.

The period is really a very long one.  It began with isolated cries for reform like those of Wycliffe in England and Huss in Germany uttered by members of the Church itself. Then came years of intense unrest, during which there was nothing so sacred that it was not argued in the street, and no point of theology, however difficult, that was not discussed in the tavern or at the market fairs. Still later, the Western Church became rent asunder and its parts waged war one against another. Then, lastly, the English Church, by this time isolated from the rest of Christendom, was forced to struggle for its very existence and came out of the contest only half triumphant, for its victory was accompanied by large secessions from its ranks. Something of the general European history of each part of the period needs to be known if the final result in England is to be understood.

The movement as we have seen began with Wycliffe, who with unsparing vigour had exposed the corruptions of the Papal Court and had denounced many of the doctrines of the Medieval Church. For a time, however, the question of reform in England was put into the background, owing first to its association with politics, and then to the outbreak of those Wars of the Roses which, while they lasted, occupied all the energies of the ruling classes. But elsewhere the result was

different. The marriage of Richard II. of England
with Anne of Bohemia had attracted many
Bohemian students to Oxford, and these men we
know carried back with them Wycliffe's writings,
and found for them so warm. a welcome at the
hands of John Huss and Jerome of Prague that
the authorities deemed it necessary to discuss the
matter at the great Council of Constance in 1415.
The result of that discussion, though, only proved
that so far there was no general cry for any
reforms in doctrine. The teaching of Wycliffe
was condemned, and Huss and Jerome were both
burnt for refusing to recant. But it was impossible
that the matter should end in that way. The
Papal influence had eagerly sought for the
condemnation of the new views, yet to every
demand for the reform of the Papal Court itself,
or for any alterations in institutions which
ministered to its greed of power or wealth, it
offered a stubborn and persecuting resistance, and
it was because such treatment was uniformly
meted out to those who agitated for such
reform that men in general began to do what
Wycliffe had previously done by himself. They
began to question whether the Papal influence
need be maintained at all, and as the authority of

the Church seemed to be dependent upon that of
the Papacy they were inclined to throw that over
also, and to have recourse to the Scriptures as the
only really trustworthy guide.  Matters were only
made worse by the fact that just at this time, when
the Church most needed wise and true leaders, the
seat of the Popes was occupied by a succession of
Pontiffs unfitted in every way for their position.
Some of them were of infamous character, some
were utterly worldly, some weak and time-serving.
Never had the need of a central guiding-power
been so widely felt, and never had the claim of the
Popes to be such a power been put forward more
boldly, and yet never before had the Popes been so
unworthy.

Yet we shall be altogether in the wrong if we
imagine that at this particular time it was only
the personal character of the Popes which produced
the general cry for reform.  That cry owed its
origin to other causes also.

First there was the discovery of the art of
printing, the art by means of which copies of
treatises are rapidly multiplied and enormously
cheapened.  What telegraphy has done in our
own time for the world at large, printing did
in that age for Europe: it brought the different

nations of Europe into close touch one with another.

Also, just at the time when this power of making many books was invented, there arose throughout Europe a new passion for knowledge due to the coming into Italy of a continual stream of Greek scholars, a stream which reached its full force upon the capture of Constantinople by Sultan Mohammed II. on May 29, 1453. To most of us Constantinople is only the name of the chief city of the Turkish Empire. But 460 years ago it was the one great seat of Christian learning. It was a Greek city, where · the knowledge of the great Greek authors had never been lost. When at last it fell its scholars fled to Italy to earn a livelihood by the teaching of their native language. They did not come without good grounds for their hope that they would be well received, but none of them dreamt how great would be the result of their coming. Through them the nations of the West felt for the first time the power of Greek thought, the loftiness of the best Greek morality, and the wonderfulness of Greek beauty. But though the things taught by the new teachers produced great results, the spirit of their teaching became even of more importance, since it was a spirit of free inquiry making a claim for the fullest liberty to discuss all subjects, even the most sacred, and asserting that nothing should be taught or held as an article of Faith which could not stand the keenest scrutiny. Under the influence of this spirit Erasmus, the greatest scholar of the age, examined the Decretals upon which the whole fabric of the Medieval Papacy with all its far-reaching claims had been constructed, with the result that soon the world learnt that many of those Decretals were altogether false, whilst others, though not false in themselves, had been given a false importance by being ascribed to Bishops of Rome of the first and second centuries, instead of to their real authors who had lived in far later ages. People found for the first time that the Apostles and their immediate successors knew nothing of the Papacy inasmuch as no Papacy had been in existence then, and so their old respect for the Papacy as an institution possessing Divine authority began to vanish away, and they came to regard its dominion as a tyranny based upon usurpation, and therefore to demand its destruction.

So far England was at one with the rest of Europe. But on the Continent a revolt from the

Papacy was only too often accompanied by a revolt from the Church as well. The claims of Plato as a teacher were set up against those of Christ, and the Christian Faith with its demands upon conduct was openly disregarded. The New Learning, however, did not have this latter effect in England. English scholars welcomed it as a power by means of which the Church's teaching would be understood more thoroughly and the lessons of purity and self-denial better enforced upon a worldly clergy. William Warham, Archbishop of Canterbury, Thomas More, Lord Chancellor, and John Colet, Dean of S. Paul's, were all of them notable scholars of the New Learning, and they were all devoutly-minded men. The spirit of the new age in Italy showed itself at its best in Leo X., who became Pope in 1513. Encouraged by him, the fine arts flourished in Italy as they had never flourished before. But while he did this, Leo also tolerated the open sale of indulgences and pardons for enormous and disgraceful crimes. On the other hand, the spirit of the new age in England is seen in Colet, who devoted a fortune left him by his father to the founding of S. Paul's School in London, putting over the entrance of it the figure of the Child Jesus with the motto 'Hear ye Him,' and adding in his statutes that his intent by this school was ' specially to increase knowledge, and worshipping of God and our Lord Jesus Christ, and good Christian life and manners in children.' To Leo it seemed that the New Learning contributed to the pleasure of life; to Colet it was a means by which life might be made more noble. For the Italian it supplied the place of theology; for the Englishman it made theology the most deeply fascinating of all studies. What is true of Colet was equally true of his companions. Sir Thomas More, for instance, was a man equally in earnest, equally devout, equally zealous for the New Learning. He was a man, his son-in-law was able to say, ' of singular virtue and of a clear unspotted conscience, more pure, I think, than the whitest snow.' If his wife or any of his children had been sick or troubled, he would tell them: ' We may not look at our pleasure to go to heaven in fether beddes—it is not the way. For our Lord Himselfe went thither with grete pains and by many tribulations . . . and the servant may not look to be in better case than his Master.'

The character, however, of the followers of the New Learning in England is not our main concern. What we have to bear in mind is that just when printing was invented there was also a notable increase in the number of the scholars who could make use of the new art, and by the combined influence of this new art and this new race of teachers, a wide public was being prepared by the spread of a more accurate knowledge, especially of the Bible itself, to take part in the settlement of religious questions.

Meanwhile another event took place which also had its effect in the quickening of the pulse of Europe. A new world was discovered when Columbus sailing westwards found in 1492 the West Indian Islands. The effect of this discovery was startling. Europe came into contact with new faiths and new races of men. It had been asserted by men of old time that the Pope and Emperor were like the sun and moon, and that they both had been appointed by God to govern the world. Yet Columbus made known to an astonished Church that there were people in existence who had never acknowledged any Emperor as overlord, and who knew nothing of the faith of the Pope; and men soon began to ask one another what became of the Pope's claim to be God's Vicegerent of all people upon earth, and, further, that if the Papal claims were seen to be without foundation in one direction, might they not equally be without foundation in other directions?

And how closely together in point of time all these events took place! The art of printing was invented in 1440. The city of Constantinople was taken in 1453. America began to be discovered in 1492. Is it to be wondered at that the whole of Europe, England included, was soon in a state of religious ferment?

But England was also profoundly influenced by yet another event. During this same period—during this same second half of the fifteenth century, the country was disturbed by a civil war which had far other results than the mere slaughter of some thousands of men.

The first battle of the Wars of the Roses was fought at S. Albans in 1455, the last on Bosworth Field in 1485. During those thirty years the old order changed—feudalism disappeared; the old race of great territorial lords, each of them a small King in his own domains, vanished away; and Henry VII. found himself a King over a nation, if not, indeed, of shopkeepers, yet of small squires and merchants. Nominally the Wars of the Roses was a struggle between two branches of the royal House of Plantagenet for the possession of the

Crown. In reality it was an outbreak of feudal anarchy, an outbreak which might at any time be expected, and which, in fact, always did occur whenever there might happen to be upon the throne either a weak King or one whose title was open to question. The struggle, moreover, showed how little removed, either in power or in theory, the King was from the great nobles around him. He was a lord over lords rather than a King over subjects. At the best he was only the greatest, the most powerful Baron, while not seldom the Barons surpassed him in splendour, and always received within their own domain a greater homage than was ever paid there to their nominal sovereign. It is evident that there could be no development of national life so long as such powerful elements within it remained uncontrolled.

The monarchy, however, was never called upon to destroy the Barons, for the Barons destroyed themselves. Every battle in the Wars of the Roses meant the lessening of their numbers. If there was an interval in actual fighting then there was many a judicial murder, and when the end of the struggle came in 1485 it came because the fighters were dead. There was barely a castle which had not to mourn the loss of its chief. The pettiness of the

rebellions of Lambert Simnel and Perkin Warbeck
in the reign of Henry VII. is due far more to the
fact that the opposing leaders had been destroyed
rather than that the new King was especially beloved
or especially capable. For 100 years indeed from
the fighting on Bosworth Field there was no check
upon the sovereign power in England. The whole
of the sixteenth century was a period of pure
despotism when the government of the Tudors
was far more unconstitutional in spirit, if not
always so in form, than was ever that of Charles I.
or James II. It was a period during which there
was but one dangerous rising against the Government, for the noble class—that is, the class that
had been trained to face the royal power in open
opposition—had disappeared, while the new class—
the middle class of small gentry and business folk
and yeoman farmers, who, in the following century
were to be seen opposing the sovereign power with
even greater vigour and with much more startling
success than the nobles had ever done—that class
had not yet risen into importance. The interest of
this fact for us now is that because of it Henry VIII.
and the Council of Regency in the time of
Edward VI. had an uncontrolled power to deal
with the affairs of the Church as well as with the

affairs of the State.   If the Baronage had not disappeared, Henry VIII. might still perhaps have
put away his wife Katharine, but he certainly
would not have been allowed to dissolve the
monasteries, whilst the dark days of Edward VI.—
perhaps as dark as any through which England has
yet lived—would scarcely have arisen, for the unscrupulous men of that time would have received
short shrift at the hands of the Barons.   Parliaments, indeed, were called throughout the whole
period, but they were regarded merely as convenient instruments for giving legal form to the
royal will, for masking tyranny under the forms of
law.   The franchise in the boroughs was, as a rule,
in the hands of a very few ; bribery and intimida-
tion were commonly resorted to if there was the
least danger of opposition to a candidate who was
known to favour the royal views ; and if, even
after the use of such means, a sufficient majority
seemed still to be doubtful, then enfranchisement
was extended to other places which could be
depended upon to return the kind of man required.

But the Wars of the Roses did more than
destroy the only class which could then offer an
effective resistance to the King.   They also caused
the merchants and farmers to throw themselves

11

into the royal arms, since the turbulent Baron was a
terror to both one class and the other.  To such
men civil faction meant ruin.  It was impossible to
produce wool or corn whilst the land was being
overrun by armed bands of men, and yet without
wool and corn they were deprived of their chief
articles of exchange.  Even in times of so-called
peace they saw little of the power of the King, but
much of that of the great lords, and this latter was
sufficiently oppressive to make them wish to be
rid of it.  A distant King, even with more
arbitrary power, might be an easier burden to bear
than a lord always in the neighbourhood with a
disorderly body of followers at his beck and call.
So they longed for a strong Government which
would enforce the peace, and they were prepared
to pay a good price for it if it could be got.  Hence
their joy when Henry VII. on his accession
married Elizabeth Woodville the Yorkist; hence
their acquiescence in the rule of Henry VIII.
As a whole they had few ideals beyond that of
succeeding in business.  If the King so ordered
public affairs that they could make money, well
and good ; they would then loyally support him.
The only reason why they dreaded the putting
away of Queen Katharine was that they thought it

might have an ill effect upon the wool-trade with Flanders ! From such men it was not difficult to obtain a House of Commons which would be always duly subservient to the King.

We have now seen in outline what was the condition of Europe generally and of England in particular at the beginning of the reign of Henry VIII. The reform in the Church, so eagerly desired by all the best men of every nation during the past hundred years, was surely nearer its accomplishment than ever before. True, the great obstacle was the Papacy itself, but people did not despair of getting some Pope to summon a General Council which should have authority to decide questions of faith and morals. A hundred years earlier a Pope had submitted to a General Council, and why should not the sixteenth century be as fortunate as the fifteenth century had been ? This hope of better days was beginning to possess the Church when quite suddenly Europe was startled by the report of a matter which was recognized as serious from the very first, and which, on reflection, was seen to involve the prospect of many and wide-spread complications. The King of England, upon whom the Head of the Church had only recently conferred the title of Defender of the Faith, was said to be at variance with His Holiness on the question of his marriage.  Henry declared that he had scruples of conscience about the matter.  In reality he had become fascinated by 'the black-blue Irish hair and Irish eyes' of Anne Boleyn.

# CHAPTER VI

## POLITICAL REFORMATION

IT was the marriage question which was the cause of Henry's estrangement with the Bishop of Rome. We ought not to forget that the people of England were devoutly attached to the Catholic Church, and of no one was this more true than it was of Henry VIII. himself. The Henry who in 1534 secured the repudiation of the Papal authority in England was the same, so far as his religious views were concerned, as the Henry who, thirteen years before, had written the attack upon Luther. The King had not changed his views—he had only been unable to secure from the Pope a decree in favour of the nullity of his marriage with Katharine. He was then, as before, satisfied with the current teaching of the Church, and he remained so practically until his death. And this feeling of satisfaction he shared in common with the best men in England at the time. It is an error only too commonly held that the repudiation of the Papal authority in England was caused by a vast mass of Protestant feeling, and that the Statutes of 1533 and 1534 were carried on the crest of a wave of a great popular enthusiasm directed against the doctrines that up to that time had been taught by the Church. Nothing could be more untrue. There was no strong Protestant sentiment in existence in England then at all. The repudiation of the Papal authority was, indeed, on the whole very popular ; it had always been desired by the English Church, whose earlier history shows it in successful resistance to Rome, and whose later history before the sixteenth century records only its unwilling subjection. But the repudiation of the Papal authority was one thing ; the rejection of certain parts of the then accepted teaching of the Western Church was quite another. No one who desires to understand the sixteenth century must regard these as only two names for the same thing. They are not two names for one thing—they are two names for two things. In other words, it was possible to break with the Papacy without breaking with the Catholic Church. But however glad the National Church might be at the prospect of regaining its freedom from foreign control, it had little cause to be grateful to the King through whose action the freedom came. Henry took up the matter for a purely personal reason: he desired to be rid of his wife. One would gladly pass over altogether. if it were possible, what is perhaps the most discreditable incident in English history. It is only mentioned here because of its bearings on the wider question of the day. Speaking strictly, Henry did not sue for a divorce, for to sue for a divorce means that the original legality of the marriage is taken for granted, but that something or other has occurred since which justifies the applicant, in his opinion, in asking that the original bond may be annulled. Moreover, a decree of divorce would not have met Henry's case at all, for such a decree carried with it no right to marry again ; but to marry again was just what Henry wished to do. His request was that the original marriage contract with Katharine might be declared by a competent authority—*i.e.*, by the Bishop of Rome—to be null and void from the very first. We need not stop to estimate the degree of moral wickedness shown by Henry. We need only remember that in those days appeals were constantly being made to Rome for decrees

of nullity of marriage, and that such appeals were
seldom refused—scarcely, indeed, ever refused if
sufficient money were forthcoming to pay for them,
and it is certain that Henry was totally unpre-
pared for any opposition to his wishes.  Why,
then, was this appeal not granted ?  Why was not
the course which had been observed in so many
other cases adopted here ?  In the answer to these
questions lies the reason why the King forced on
the repudiation by England of the Papal Supremacy.  The Pope did not grant the decree of
nullity asked for because he was afraid of the
Queen's nephew, Charles V., the Emperor.  The
Pope acted from political advantage, but the
political advantage he thought of was not that
of England but that of the Empire ; and England,
realizing that the Pope was but a tool in the hand
of Charles V., resented his action accordingly.
English people, said the late Bishop Creighton, felt
that if dirty work was to be done at all the dirty
work of the English King deserved doing as much
as that of anyone else.  The Pope cursed Henry
in his heart, not because he had applied for a
decree of nullity, but because he happened to want
such a decree which, if granted, would infallibly
bring the Papacy into conflict with the Emperor.

So every possible delay was made use of. The case was first tried in England, and then called to Rome, whither also Henry was summoned to show cause why his request should be granted. This summons opened the eyes of the English people; they began to see that the Papal claims involved the subordination of the National Sovereign as well as that of the National Church, and they were indignant that their King should be called upon to go to Rome as an inferior and vassal of the Pope.

But what could be done? Neither side wished to bring the quarrel to a crisis, but as time went on the King in various ways tried to compel the Pope to give way. Thus in the spring of 1532 there was passed an Act for the restraint of the payment of annates. These annates were fines to the value of one year's income, which, by long custom, were paid to the Pope by anyone newly admitted to a benefice, and the Act gave the King the power of saying that these should no longer be paid. It is not difficult to see that the real intention of the Act was to put into Henry's hands an instrument by means of which he could coerce the Pope into doing as he wished.

All things at this time seemed to favour the

12

King's suit. Not only did a subservient Parliament pass legislation as the King willed, but also towards the end of the same year 1532 there occurred a vacancy in the Archbishopric of Canterbury, and the King secured the appointment of Thomas Cranmer, a man who was known to be on the King's side on the great marriage question. To open a way for the new Archbishop to proceed with the case, an Act had been passed dealing with appeals to Rome, which declared that all causes from henceforth should be settled within the King's jurisdiction and authority; and that if the Pope should lay the country under an Interdict by reason of this Act, yet the clergy were to take no notice of any such Interdict under pain of imprisonment and fine. So Cranmer, having fixed his court at Dunstable as a place conveniently removed from any great centre of population, cited the Queen to appear, but she, of course, ignored the whole proceedings. Then on May 23, 1534, it was formally announced that in the opinion of the court the marriage of the King with Katharine of Arragon had all along been invalid; in other words, that the King had during the whole of this period been in a position to marry someone else. Six days later it was further decreed that the marriage which Henry had already privately contracted with Anne Boleyn was a valid and legal one.

The King had achieved his purpose. He had worked his way through all obstacles by sheer force of will. He did not, however, discontinue his anti-Papal legislation. Such earlier Acts as had been conditional were now made operative; provision was made for the election of Archbishops and Bishops without any reference to Rome; from henceforth it became treason for any Chapter to appoint anyone to a vacancy except such man as the King had recommended; and, lastly, by an Act dealing with Papal dispensations and the payment of Peter's Pence, England was discharged finally from all financial relations with the Papal See.

Great Statutes had thus been placed upon the Rolls of Parliament with a startling rapidity, but yet it must be carefully remembered that in all this legislation Henry had so far not done anything that was new, nor had he acted in a spirit different from that which had shown itself before in the English nation, nor had he endeavoured to create a schism in the Church. The anti-Papal clauses of the Statutes of 1533 and 1534 can be matched by clauses in earlier Statutes of the realm. Then in what, it may be asked, does the importance of Henry's legislation consist? The answer is that, whereas the legislation of earlier days had, for one reason or another, been inoperative, Henry's legislation was successful and became the permanent policy of the realm. The action of earlier Kings those earlier Kings themselves had often set aside for the sake of their own interest, for though the feeling of the National Church in favour of its spiritual independence never changed, yet sometimes the Kings found it convenient to ignore the Statues of the realm and to make use of the custom of appealing to Rome. But in Henry's reign the royal interest coincided with that of the Church, and the Papal Supremacy became a thing of the past.

But though the King thus rid the Church of all foreign control he had no intention of giving it its freedom. It was farthest from his thoughts that there should be a kingdom within his kingdom. To prevent such a result he reasserted that which had always been the theory of the royal position with regard to the Church, namely, that it was the duty of the King to see that all his subjects were properly governed, not only as members of the State, but

also as members of the Church, since their persons
and their property were subject to his laws, their
souls alone being outside his control.    Moreover, as
the King was not merely the head of the State but
also the eldest son of the Church and her recognized champion, he was therefore bound to protect
her ; and so the Act of 1532 said that the King's
highness as a good Christian Prince ought to
repress the exactions of the Papal Court.    But
to the restatement of the old claims were added
new ones which threatened the very life of the
National Church.    In 1534 it was declared that
although the Sovereign was not the channel of
spiritual grace, yet he was the source of all jurisdiction, as well spiritual as civil, and that the King
had not merely the right to see that the spiritual
authorities exercised their jurisdiction, but also the
right to exercise that authority himself if he so
desired ; and, further, that the scope of the ecclesiastical jurisdiction could not be varied in any direction without the royal authority.    Henceforth the
Church might issue no new Canons except with the
royal assent.    The world might progress, the times
might change, but the Church was to remain
bound by its old rules unless the King decreed
that it might legislate for itself.    It was soon found

that there might be a worse tyranny even than that of the Popes of Rome. In the rough speech of the time, it was said that Henry was ' a King with a Pope in his belly.' But legislation of this sort, bad as it was, was not the only hindrance placed by this autocratic Sovereign upon the Church's development. Care was taken that in future only such persons should be promoted to high office within the Church as could be depended upon to acquiesce in the royal view of the Church's position. There were never in future to be any Anselms or Beckets or Langtons or Winchelseas. The National Church was to do as it was told and never to dream of giving expression to any views unless such views coincided with those of the Crown.

Still Henry was not satisfied. He had married Anne Boleyn ; he had secured the passing of very definite anti-Papal legislation ; he had reduced the National Church to a department of State. But he knew that he had lost much of his old popularity. A women's riot at Great Yarmouth about the marriage question, and the way in which the women of London whenever they saw Anne Boleyn would call her by opprobrious names, proved to him plainly that the common people were dis-

gusted with him. He had been styled ' Defensor
Fidei ' ; he ought, rather, it was said, to be called
' Destructor Fidei.' So with characteristic energy
he tried to compel the people to be loyal ; they
as well as the clergy were not to have opinions
of their own. Hence, in the same year 1534
Parliament was made to pass the Succession Act,
which not only declared that the marriage with
Anne Boleyn was good and agreeable to the law of
God, but also that all people should take an oath
to say that they regarded it as such. Tyranny
could scarcely go farther. Such legislation was
intolerable, and it is not strange that the best men
preferred to die rather than submit to it. Both
Sir Thomas More, the noblest spirit in Europe at
the time, and the saintly Bishop Fisher became
martyrs for conscience' sake. Their opposition had
been expected indeed, and so soon as they were seen
to be disobedient they were thrown into prison.
But in their case at least the King seemed afraid to
proceed to extremities. He hoped to the last that
they would yield, and his counsel tried every possible means to secure their submission. Their fate
in the end was probably brought about by the
conduct of a new Pope, Paul III., who celebrated
his election to the Papal Chair by the creation of

seven new Cardinals, one of the seven being John
Fisher. Henry was angry at this beyond measure,
brutally declaring that Fisher should wear his
Cardinal's cap upon his shoulders, and with little
more ado both Bishop and ex-Chancellor were
put to death. Such action naturally increased the
King's unpopularity, but, as his unpopularity grew,
the King became more and more determined to
crush it. He knew that there was much murmur-
ing, especially within the walls of the religious
houses, and, therefore, making use of the powers
now vested in him by Act of Parliament, he
made one Thomas Cromwell, a clever unprincipled
lawyer, his Vicar-General, and gave him instruc-
tions to 'visit' immediately the religious orders.
Visitation hitherto had meant an inquiry as to
how far a religious body was obeying its own
constitution. It now, however, gave absolute
power to the Visitor, acting on rules known only
to himself, either to reform a community or to
do away with it altogether.

This official visitation began in 1535, but the
result of it was determined upon ere it began
inasmuch as the King had resolved upon the
destruction of the whole monastic system. The
independent attitude of the monks irritated him,

whilst their wealth excited his greed. But here
again the royal purpose was to be achieved by
process of law; Parliament was to decree that
the religious houses ought to be done away
with. The first step towards this end was the
obtaining of a sufficiently bad report as to the
state of the houses, and this was duly furnished
by three Commissioners who had been carefully
chosen by Cromwell as men likely to do this disgraceful work in a fitting manner. Then, in order
that the Parliament might be induced to accept
the report without too close an examination into
its truthfulness, and upon it might pass the necessary legislation without opposition, it was loudly
whispered everywhere that the legislators would
be allowed to share in the plunder. Such a prospect at any time would prove dangerously alluring,
but at that particular moment it was irresistible,
for many of the gentry were in as great a state
of impecuniosity as was the King himself, the
extravagant Court life of Henry's earlier years and
the lavish display at the Field of the Cloth of
Gold having reduced many a courtier almost to
beggary. So soon, therefore, as it became known
that the destruction of the religious houses had
been determined upon, letters of request for grants

of land began to pour in upon Cromwell from all sides, and when the reports furnished by Cromwell's Commissioners were read in Parliament there were of course cries of " Down with them, down with them, even to the ground."

The whole monastic system did not, indeed, go at once, the lesser monasteries being at first the only ones affected. The Act compelling their dissolution said that the King was influenced only by a desire for the true glory and honour of God, and that because the greater monasteries, within which " religion was right well kept and observed," were not full, therefore the members of the smaller monasteries ought to be sent to them. From beginning to end the Act is a monument of hypocrisy.

These proceedings led to a rebellion on the part of the people; the King at last had gone too far even for him, and civil war again seemed imminent. Especially serious was the outbreak in Yorkshire where an army of 30,000 insurgents had gathered prepared to do battle for the religious houses. The danger, however, disappeared almost as quickly as it had arisen, for the rebels, trusting in the promise of the King that their grievances should be favourably considered, broke up their ranks and

went home, only to see the King almost immediately afterwards proceeding to lay hands upon
their leaders and using their rising as an excuse
for the suppression of the greater religious houses.
Again was seen the same travesty of justice and
the same disregard for every principle of right
conduct.    There still exists in Cromwell's own
handwriting the following note, with regard to
Abbot Richard Whiting, of Glastonbury : " Item :
the Abbot of Glaston to be tried at Glaston, and
also executed there ; " with another which says
that care was to be taken that the evidence for
the Abbot's trial was to be " well sorted."

The confiscation of the property of the monastic
houses was attended by gross wastefulness and by
a complete disregard for the value of everything
that could not be changed at once into money ;
priceless objects of art were destroyed ; the books
of the libraries were scattered broadcast ; even the
screens of the churches were used to make the
fires by which was melted down the lead that had
been stripped from off the roof.    Still more serious
were the results of this spoliation in other directions.    The old religious houses had been the chief
agencies for the relief of the poor and for the care
of the sick, whilst such education as existed then

was in their hands, and it was through them that poor lads passed to the Universities; but when their destruction was accomplished all organized effort for the care of the country people came to an end, whilst the establishment of a few grammar schools in the provincial towns was but a sorry substitute for the many monastic schools which they were said to replace. The poor in England have never known so sad a time, either before or since, as the fifty years which followed upon the dissolution of the monasteries. Included also in the confiscation were, of course, all those tithes which of right belonged to the parishes served by the vicars of the monastic houses, but which the monasteries had been accustomed to keep for themselves. The monasteries had acted as robbers of parish endowments, and now the King and his courtiers became the receivers of the stolen goods.

This suppression of the religious orders meant the removal of the last hindrance to the tyrannical power of the King. The nobles had disappeared in the Wars of the Roses. The mitred Abbots and the great friars were now gone as well. The King was left alone. The rest of his reign and the reign of his son were years of absolute despotism, the darkest period in the whole of English history.

As we look back we can see how harmful was the result of Henry's policy upon the National Church. She was maimed in almost every limb by him who bore the title of Defender of the Faith. It was not simply that he robbed her of her money, nor yet that he tried to make her a mere department of State. Worse than all else he destroyed her best men. By his legislation he had decreed that the Church of England should stand alone and should decide matters of faith and worship without reference to the rest of western Christendom ; but by his tyranny he also destroyed just those men who in such a crisis might have guided her wisely and safely through all the dangers that were bound to meet her.

Henry had sworn at his coronation in 1509 to preserve his people's liberties and to defend their Church. Before he came to die his people were wellnigh slaves and their Church was almost gone.

# CHAPTER VII

WHEN Henry died in January 1547 his son Edward had but recently kept his ninth birthday. When death seemed near the King showed his distrust of the men into whose hands he had perforce to leave the care of his son by preparing a will in which he carefully stated that no further change should be made in either Church or State until the young Edward should reach the age of sixteen and should then be declared to be of age. But these men, trained by the example of Henry himself to disregard every principle of honour, set the King's will on one side immediately, made Somerset Protector of the Realm, and proceeded to deal with public affairs as it seemed best to them. For more than four years Somerset governed in the name of the boy-King, and then his place was taken by Dudley, Duke of Northumberland, who had been for a long time plotting against his authority, and who finally succeeded in obtaining his execution. The change of masters was, if possible, a change for the worse. Somerset had been a thief; he had reaped much profit out of the dissolution of the Chantries; he had made an attempt to pull down first S. Margaret's, Westminster, and then the Abbey, in order to build his house in the Strand at as little a cost to himself as possible; and when his house was built he robbed S. Paul's of its books to furnish his library. But besides being a thief he tried to be an autocrat and he fell because he kept himself aloof from the remainder of the Council. Yet Somerset was a respectable man in comparison with Northumberland. Northumberland stuck at nothing which could minister to his own selfish ends—treachery, lying, robbery, judicial murder, treason—he was guilty of them all in turn. Religion for him was a mere matter of policy. If he had any belief at all it was in the old ways rather than in the new, and yet, when it seemed to suit his ends, he posed as an extreme reformer and made John Knox his chaplain. It was well for England that by the boy-King's death this man's authority extended over only two years.

But under both Protectors the National Church

suffered grievously. Confiscation had grown almost into a custom; personal greed or the supposed necessities of the nation were quite sufficient reasons for laying hands upon ecclesiastical property. At last the order was given that even the parish churches were to be robbed of their valuables, and it is still possible for almost every parish in the land, however insignificant or remote, to see for itself in the accounts in the Public Record Office in what way the Royal Commissioners visited it and took away the bells out of the church-tower, and the vestments from the presses, and stripped the altars of their hangings.

But there was other work done in the name of religion in the reign of Edward VI. which was of far greater consequence than the mutilation of the fabrics of the churches and the confiscation of their goods. Attempts were made to alter completely the character of the worship enacted within them. No changes had occurred in this direction during the whole reign of Henry except that by an Act of Parliament passed a few years before his death the first step was taken to secure a uniformity of worship throughout England by ordering that the Use of Sarum should be the Use for the whole province of Canterbury, in other words, for what was then by far the more important part of England. Other changes, however, were known to be in preparation, and to understand them a word or two is required to describe the character of the worship which was then in existence. It was commonly the custom for the parish priests to say Matins in church at 6 or 6.30 a.m. ; Mass, as the Eucharistic service was universally called, was said at 9 or 9.30 ; and Evensong came at 2 p.m., or thereabouts. Of these the services which the parishioners themselves attended were Mass and Evensong. The language in which all the services were said was Latin, yet, nevertheless, the services were more helpful to the common people than it seems possible at first sight they could have been. The service of the Mass especially was filled with symbolical acts the significance of which was undoubtedly understood. The solemn approach of the priest to the altar, the frequent censings, the ringing of the sanctus bell at the Consecration, the elevation of the Host, the passing round of the peace board for all the people to kiss —these were the things by which the worshippers were taught what the service meant. Books also, such as the 'Lay Folks' Mass Book,' contained devotions in the English tongue for the use of

14

the people at the time of the Celebration, like
the manuals which are so largely in use for a
similar purpose to-day.  Yet, although the old
services were far other than meaningless forms to
the people, there was undoubtedly great room for
reform.  Especially was it needful to make the
Mass a service in which the people should be
taught to communicate as well as one in which
they should meet for worship.  This great end
was secured by the Order for Communion which
was put forth in 1548.  In the following year was
published what is known as the First Prayer-Book
of Edward VI., and this completed the work of
the Committee appointed by Henry to deal with
the public services of the National Church.  The
object which that Committee had in view was to
maintain as far as possible the character and tone
of the old services, but to make them more simple
and to have them rendered in the vulgar tongue
so that every possible opportunity might be given
to the people to take an intelligent share in them.
When, however, this Prayer-Book is compared
with the old Service Books one point stands out
with a significance which was unnoticed indeed at
the time but which has been realized later.  The
old Service Books were prepared for the use of

the clergy and they are therefore full of the most careful directions as to the way in which the services should be performed.   These directions seem to us now to have erred in being too elaborate and precise, but they did secure at least that the services should be rendered with solemnity and care.   The new Prayer-Book, on the other hand, was put forth for the use of the people, and consequently ritual directions for the officiating priests scarcely found any place in it at all, the idea being that the old customary ways would continue.   But as time went on the number of those who had been educated in the old ways grew less and less, and as their places were taken by others who had received no guidance in the method of conducting the public services save such as were contained in the Prayer-Book itself, the old customs almost died out and were replaced by others which varied with the prepossessions of each new incumbent. It was ignorance rather than prejudice which thus led to the disuse of the old ceremonial.   In all other essentials the new Prayer - Book consisted of the old services in a new dress.   But even so it was received with very little favour by the nation.   The people in the West, indeed, rose in rebellion against the attempt to enforce its use upon them.  Undeterred, however, by such signs of popular feeling, the Duke of Northumberland on becoming Protector sanctioned the preparation of a second Prayer-Book, doing so because he needed for other ends of his the support of the extreme reform party in England.  This second book when it was issued in 1552 was seen at once to involve the most serious consequences. The old religion was henceforth to be done away with, and a new one representing the views of the extreme Foreign Protestant party was to be substituted for it.  The most startling changes were to be found naturally in the service of the Holy Communion.  Here the alterations involved both a denial of the sacrificial aspect of the Eucharist and also of the Real Presence.  Moreover, not in this service only but throughout the whole book there was felt to be a new tone.  In the old services in the First Prayer-Book the people were encouraged to come as children into the presence of their Heavenly Father to render Him willing homage.  In this new book they were taught to come as servants conscious of the many and grievous offences which they had committed against their Sovereign Lord.

This Second Prayer-Book was the crowning

achievement of Northumberland's Protectorate.
What did the nation think of him and of all his
works ? The answer to that question is to be
found in the tumultuous joy with which the
Princess Mary was welcomed as Queen.

Mary was known to be an ardent Papalist,
but, in spite of that, she came to the throne possessing the devotion of her people to a degree
which few other Sovereigns have shared in. Yet
this accession of the daughter of Katharine of
Arragon presented the greatest difficulties to the
great mass of English Church people. They
abhorred the attempts of the extreme reformers to
cut the National Church adrift from the old ways,
and yet they were by no means desirous of being
brought again under the control of the Papacy.
No other course, however, seemed to be open to
them. To throw in their lot with the Protestants
involved the acceptance of a new Faith and rather
than do that they acquiesced in the revival of the
old Papal tyranny. That was, indeed, the lesser
evil of the two, but as a consequence of it there
were from that time onward only two parties in
the National Church, each being a party of
extremists : the great middle party—the party
which had rejoiced in the abolition of Papal

domination while retaining the old Catholic faith and worship, and which had found its views expressed in the first Prayer-Book—this party was forced by the pressure of events to throw in its lot with that Papalist party which until now had been comparatively unimportant.

Mary reigned till 1558, and when she died there can be little doubt that the people were as glad to hear of her death as they had been five years before to hear of her coronation. She had begun her reign by securing the repeal of all the great ecclesiastical Statutes of her father and brother, and the Houses of Parliament, in the name of the country, had been made to seek absolution from the Papacy for their recent conduct. Affairs were thus restored to the condition in which they had been before 1534, except that the Queen found, to her bitter disappointment, that it was impossible to get the laity to surrender the Church lands of which they were now possessed. Then came her marriage with Philip II. of Spain. The first news of such an alliance was received by her people with marked dislike, but the Queen hoped too much from it to be thwarted in her project. To her it seemed the means of making secure for ever the new allegiance of her people to the Papacy ; for if she should

become by this marriage the happy possessor of a
son, that son would inherit a vast Empire every
part of which acknowledged the Papal supremacy,
and England would be part of a great confederacy
to uphold the true Faith.  But it was just this
possibility of the country being swamped in the
great dominions of the Spanish King which made
Englishmen dislike the match so much.  Mary
herself was half Spanish, and any child of Mary
and Philip would be three parts a Spaniard, and
would, it was feared, regard his English possessions
as a mere appendage of his great Empire.  The
marriage, however, did not bring to the Queen
any of the happy results she had so fondly hoped
for.  Philip remained in England only a few
weeks, and even during that time treated his wife
with a coldness which touched her to the quick ;
while as the months went on it became evident that
she would never become a mother.  With her
naturally somewhat morbid disposition she told
herself that these sore trials were the judgment of
Heaven upon her for her want of diligence in
destroying the heresy which she knew to be so
prevalent within her kingdom.  To appease the
Divine wrath and to win by acts of a deeper devotion the blessings she so ardently longed for, she

entered upon that course of persecution which has made her reign so terrible a one in the annals of England.  The market-places of all the great towns were lit up with the fires which burnt the heretics. The more noble the personal character of the heretic the more need that he should be put to death ; and the greater the dislike of the people for such measures was only a greater proof that such measures were required.  So things went on for the remaining three years during which Mary's reign lasted, and little as it is possible to approve of the policy she adopted, it is yet possible to sympathize with her in her loneliness.  Neglected by the husband she had welcomed so warmly, hated by the people whose cheers at her coronation she still remembered, and punished by the God whose anger nothing seemed to appease, she died conscious that she had failed in every direction.

# CHAPTER VIII

MARY was succeeded by Elizabeth, the daughter
of Anne Boleyn. The circumstance of the new
Queen's birth was of itself sufficient to create
serious dangers, for, as she well knew, a great part
of the nation regarded her as the living witness of
her father's unholy passion for one of the women of
his Court; while those who acknowledged her
legitimacy were just those extreme reformers who
at Mary's death came hurrying back from exile and
who, by their extravagant demands for a purer form
of religion, only increased the bitterness of party
feeling. Added to this, there was a possibility—
even a probability—of an invasion from abroad.
Philip might claim England either as the husband
of the late Queen or as a descendant of John of
Gaunt, and the Pope might be reckoned upon to
support him by protesting against Elizabeth being
recognized as a lawful child of Henry VIII. In

France, too, there was Mary of Scotland, wife of
the heir to the French Crown, and who, by virtue
of her descent from Henry VII., claimed to be the
rightful Queen of England, and whose claim all
ardent Papalists believed in.   From whatever point
of view the situation was regarded it was seen to
be fraught with the very gravest peril, and Elizabeth
therefore proceeded with extreme caution.   One
thing above all else was felt to be needful both
by herself and by the advisers whom she gathered
round her throne—namely, the adoption of a line of
policy which should bring together in as close a
harmony as possible the various parties in the
nation.   Only a united England could hope to
resist with success any interference from abroad.
A beginning in this direction was made by dealing
with all extremists in religion.   On the one hand
a new Act of Supremacy was passed which, by
vesting all ecclesiastical jurisdiction in the Crown,
defined the Queen's attitude to the Papacy, but
also, on the other hand, all unlicensed preaching
was forbidden.   Then came the issue and enforcement of a new Book of Common Prayer—a book
which in form was seen to be the second book of
Edward VI., but which in its teaching was so
different from its model as to make it possible for

the National Church to accept it. In this matter of public worship the Queen's wish in reality was to get back to the condition of things which had existed at her father's death, but she had the wisdom to see that any attempt to do that at the moment would only lose her the support of the whole Puritan party. With her policy thus clearly expressed, it only remained for her to find men both in Church and State who would loyally carry it out. Above all there was need for a wise and moderate Archbishop, and the Queen, knowing this, chose Matthew Parker for the office, and compelled him to accept it in spite of his manifest unwillingness. In many ways Parker's antecedents especially fitted him for his arduous task : he had been chaplain to Anne Boleyn, and so was peculiarly bound to Elizabeth ; as a friend of Bilney, Latimer, and Martin Bucer, he was well thought of by the Puritans ; as a student, especially of the early Fathers, he had no sympathy with the intolerance of the newly returned exiles ; and, moreover, his character was equal to his scholarship. During the sixteen years of his Archiepiscopate—perhaps the most critical years the National Church has yet experienced—he fought against bitter Calvinism on the one hand and equally bitter Papalism on the other, striving

all the while for the vindication of that middle
and yet Catholic position which is the glory of
Anglicanism. He desired, he said, to see revived
that ' most holy and Godly form of discipline which
was commonly used in the primitive Church,' and
the measure of success which he achieved is to be
seen in the Thirty-nine Articles of Religion which
were put forth whilst he was Archbishop and which,
in their present form, are mainly his work.

There was real need at the time for the English
Church to define her position, for it was evident
that the Papacy was being urged to deal decisively
with England. The Council of Trent had been
finally closed in December 1563. This Council
had been called by the Popes, not because they
wished for it in the first instance, but because they
were driven to it by the Emperor Charles V. It
was called to consider the demands of the
Reformers, but from the first it was either ham-
pered from arriving at any decision at all, or was so
packed with Papal nominees that its decisions became a foregone conclusion. Then, after its doors
had been closed for ten years, it was stirred into
activity again by the influence of the new Order
of Jesuits; and now, so far from trying to find
terms of accommodation which would be acceptable

to the Reformers, it created Roman Catholicism. Roman Catholicism stands for autocracy in ecclesiastical government and for certain doctrines in theology, and both these things—Roman Catholic government and Roman Catholic doctrines—found their first formal recognition in the decrees of the Council of Trent. Henceforward such members of the Catholic Church as still held to the Papacy were known as Roman Catholics, and for them there was to be no thought of accommodation with others but only an unflinching assertion of the new position and an enforcement of it, if necessary, by the power of the sword. Queen Elizabeth was speedily made to feel the effect of this new policy. On her accession in 1558 Pope Pius IV. had been prepared to recognize both her legitimacy and her Sovereign position if she on her part would recognize his Papal claims, but Pius V. in 1570 declared her illegitimate and absolved her people from their allegiance; and Jesuits began to arrive preaching both Romanism and treason until reports of rebellions and plots harassed the Queen's Ministers day by day.

But all other efforts of the Papacy become insignificant when compared with the great Armada which, blessed like the Crusades of old with the

Papal benediction, was sent forth from Spain to win England back to the true Faith. The story of the coming of that Armada and of its ultimate fate is happily too well known to need telling here, but we need to remember that the hostility shown towards England was only part of the policy pursued by the new Roman Catholicism against its opponents everywhere. Pope Gregory XIII. held a solemn service of thanksgiving when he heard the news of the terrible massacre of the Huguenots in France; a bitter reign of terrorism was instituted in the Low Countries; whilst William of Orange, the Stadtholder of Holland, was assassinated by a fanatical Roman Catholic partisan. A policy marked by such a series of events was, from the point of view of the real success of Rome, disastrous. The very savour of the Papacy came to stink in the nostrils of the people.

The defeat of the Spanish Armada marks the beginning of a new period in English political and religious history. Until then English people had lived in a constant state of apprehension. The power of Spain was known to be gigantic, and there was a general feeling that all the elements of the nation must unite against the common enemy. But when there was no longer any foreign foe to be dreaded, the internal disputes which had been in existence all along blazed out with a fierceness unknown before. The doctrines, the ceremonies, the threefold ministry of the Church, all came in for attack. Once again, however, the English Church was well served by her Archbishop. When Whitgift was promoted to Canterbury in 1583 the one condition Elizabeth made was that he should govern the Church resolutely, and never once during the remaining twenty years of her life had the Queen reason to regret her choice. Steadily and relentlessly Whitgift—her 'little black husband,' as his royal mistress sometimes called him—went on his way. Puritan doctrine he did not vex himself with for he was practically a Puritan himself, but Puritan disregard for outward order found no mercy at his hands. So he suppressed the prophesyings, and instituted a strict censorship of the Press, and got the Church courts strengthened so that they might deal the more effectively with obstinate offenders. The Archbishop felt that the clergy needed to be taught that liberty did not mean licence, and he lived long enough to teach them their lesson so well that they were beginning to be conscious of their real unity, and were finding out the strength that this knowledge gave them.

The death of the great Queen in 1603 did not at once alter the ecclesiastical or political situation, but it brought another Sovereign upon the scene who, though speedily found to share to the full in his predecessor's love of autocratic power, was also seen to possess far less political sagacity and far less power of winning the love of his subjects. But while the failure of James I. as a ruler was thus due in part to his own character, it was also due in part to the fact that everybody expected everything from him and everybody was consequently disappointed. The Recusants, as the Roman Catholics were called, hoped for more lenient treatment from the son of Mary of Scotland, whilst the Puritans hoped that as he had been brought up under Presbyterian influences there would be a cleansing of the Book of Common Prayer of all its superstitious defects.

In the hope of securing peace within the National Church, the King at the beginning of his reign called a conference at Hampton Court, and there all the various demands of the Puritan party were presented. The result of the conference did not, however, at all satisfy the extremists. To the Catechism was added the latter part which deals with the Sacraments of the Gospel, a new translation of the Bible was ordered, and a few minor changes were agreed upon; but in matters of ritual and of Church government the Puritans gained no concessions at all.

With regard to the Recusants, the King found himself in a position made the more difficult by the action of the Recusants themselves.   James wished to be lenient towards them provided he could be satisfied about their loyalty to himself.   This involved a denial on their part of the claim of the Pope to set up or depose temporal rulers.   Many of them were disposed to make this concession, but all hopes of arriving at a satisfactory compromise were ruined by the discovery of the Gunpowder Plot—a plot in which the extreme Romanists, rendered impatient and despairing by evidences of the King's shiftiness, tried to win freedom by a destruction of their enemies.   The discovery of this conspiracy only deepened the hatred of the mass of the people for the Pope and for all those who believed in the Papal claims.

From the point of view of the National Church the Recusants, however, were not by any means such a cause of serious trouble as were the Puritans.   The former were without her pale, and could be left to be dealt with by the King, the

16

Church only lending the machinery of her courts for the purpose. The latter, however, were parts of herself, and if, in dealing with them, she had to rely on the royal support, her own true right to jurisdiction would become obscured and her prosperity would come to be bound up more and more with that of the King. In such circumstances only the very wisest handling of the various questions as they arose could insure success. Elizabeth's great Archbishop, Whitgift, had died in 1604, and Bancroft, Bishop of London, had been appointed to fill his place, and, contrary to common expectation, showed as time went on a real power of winning the confidence and respect of the various elements in the Church and by that means of bringing them into closer harmony. But when on the death of Bancroft in 1610 Abbot succeeded to the chair of S. Augustine, the whole aspect of affairs was changed. Bancroft had been a statesman; Abbot was only a second-rate politician. Bancroft believed that episcopacy was a Divine institution, and, as such, an integral part of the Church's system; but Abbot was content to be regarded as though he were merely a Crown official. Such a change in leadership could only mean disaster for the Church. During his long tenure of the office—for Abbot was Archbishop for twenty-three years—there never was a moment when there was not need for the highest statesmanship, and yet, with each succeeding year, the King became more and more at variance with his subjects on great constitutional questions, and, since in religious disputes he always took the part of the Bishops against the Puritans, the people naturally came to confound the Church with the Court. The National Church came to be looked upon as the Church of a party, and that the party opposed to popular freedom. The political and religious questions became mixed up in such a way that if a man were loyal to the Church he was suspected of being disloyal to the Constitution.

But all the time that the divisions within the Church were becoming more and more accentuated, her place as an integral part of the Church Catholic, and her fidelity to the teaching of the time before schism was known, was being nobly vindicated by scholars like Jewel and Hooker and Andrewes. The work of these men had been sorely needed, for, on the one hand, the new Jesuit movement within the Roman Church produced a band of scholars who championed the cause of the Papacy with unflinching courage, whilst, on the other hand, the

teaching of men like Calvin and John Knox
seemed to endanger the very foundations of the
Church.  From both sides shrewd blows were
directed against the English Church, since she
refused to associate herself with either one party
or the other.  But if she was to live something
more was required than a mere refusal to agree to
the position taken up by others.  A vigorous life
can never be built up upon mere negations.  It
was that which was positive in the statements of
Rome and Geneva alike which won for them the
enthusiastic support of their followers, and people
began to wonder whether the doctrinal position of
the English Church could be so stated as to win for
her a devotion equally strong.  It was not long
before such doubts were for ever set at rest.  Before
the death of King James—that is, before the first
quarter of the seventeenth century had passed
away—the theological standpoint of the National
Church had been both clearly stated and splendidly
vindicated.  The writers of that time are to the
English Church what the early Fathers are to the
Church Universal.

First of these in point of time came Jewel, Bishop
of Salisbury from 1560 to 1571, who in his ' Defence
of the English Church' declared that in all that it

had done it had only returned to the teaching of the Apostles and of the old Catholic Fathers. Then in 1589 an equally definite position as against the Puritans was taken up by Bancroft (afterwards the Archbishop) in his famous sermon at S. Paul's Cross on February 9. So far very many within the English Church had said that episcopacy was merely the most convenient form of Church government, and therefore should be accepted by both Church and State; but Bancroft asserted that there could be no true Church without episcopacy, and said this so strongly that some people complained that he had made an attack upon the supremacy of the Crown.

Of far more importance still was the work of Richard Hooker. Hooker combined great scholarship with a remarkable power of imparting his knowledge to others, and yet his great work, ' The Laws of Ecclesiastical Polity,' had its origin only in the fact that he found himself called upon to defend himself from personal attack. In 1585 he had been appointed Master of the Temple. The other candidate was one Travers, a Presbyterian, and the evening lecturer at the same church. Travers continued in his position after Hooker's appointment, and proceeded to contradict in the afternoon what

Hooker had taught in the morning; and it was the sermons and other writings which Hooker composed in self-defence which were afterwards put together in the 'Polity.' In the preface (which he wrote 'to them that seek, as they term it, the reformation of the laws and orders ecclesiastical in the Church of England') he declares that his intent is to make it clear that 'for the ecclesiastical laws of this realm we are led by great reason to observe them, and yet by no necessity bound to impugn them.' This intention of his he carried out with most striking skill and yet with a great sobriety of expression. The Puritan position with regard to the authority of the Church, its assertion that the English Church needed further purifying by the doing away with such ancient rites and ceremonies as were still retained, and its opposition to episcopacy, were all dealt with in turn ; and by his constant appeal to reason Hooker compelled his opponents to acknowledge the strength of the position taken up by the English Church. There were other great scholars who shared in this great work of vindicating their Church, but it was the 'Polity' of Hooker which made the greatest impression, and of which the Churchmen of the later Elizabethan days were the most proud.

Meanwhile, during these last years of the great Tudor Queen, another divine was rapidly attracting to himself the notice of his countrymen, and winning their love by reason of the spiritual beauty of his life quite as much as he won their regard for the greatness of his learning. This man was Lancelot Andrewes, the son of a London tradesman, born in 1555 in the parish of All Hallows', Barking. Famous as a scholar at school and at Cambridge, and equally famous as a great and eloquent preacher, he might have become a Bishop before Elizabeth's death if he had been willing to surrender a portion of the episcopal income, a condition which was attached to his acceptance of the office. When, however, James became King the offer was repeated without any such unworthy condition, and he was made, though always unwilling, successively Bishop of Chichester in 1605, of Ely in 1607, and, finally, of Winchester in 1618, influencing each diocese in turn by the holiness of his life even more than by the greatness of his sermons. It was always the man more than the scholar whom men thought of and admired, and it is difficult to estimate the importance of so saintly a life in the winning for the Church and the Church's ways the reverence of large numbers of men. But the needs of the time compelled Andrewes to take up other work in addition to that which fell to him as Bishop. In the reign of Elizabeth the Church of England had been called upon mainly to defend its position against the attacks of the Puritans; now in the reign of James it was being assailed with equal vigour and with greater scholarship by the Romanists who for this purpose had enlisted the services of Bellarmine, the most notable controversialist which the Roman Church has yet produced. In reply to this new attack Andrewes not only boldly asserted the Catholic position of the English Church, but also carried the war into the enemy's camp by drawing attention to the fact that the distinctive doctrines of Rome have no better origin than that of medieval teaching and practice; and it is of interest to remember that Bellarmine never attempted to continue the controversy further, though he lived for eleven years after the publication of Bishop Andrewes' treatise.

With this work of Andrewes the task of defending the theological position of the English Church was complete. At the accession of Queen Elizabeth half a century earlier no one, not even the Church's own friends, knew exactly where she stood; they only knew that she was mistrusted and misliked by the extremists on either side.    But now she had found herself.    Called upon, in answer to the attacks made upon her, to defend her position, she had responded with a definiteness which left little to be desired.    On the one hand, as against the extreme teaching of the Protestants, she declared herself to be truly Catholic ; on the other hand, as against the extremists of the Roman Church, she said she could not but be Protestant.

There is one other point in the controversy with Rome at this time which deserves notice.    An attack was made upon the validity of English Orders by a certain otherwise obscure Anglo-Irish priest named Holywood, who invented what is known as the 'Nag's Head Fable.'    This man declared that the Bishop of Llandaff of the time had been called upon by Queen Elizabeth to consecrate Matthew Parker as Archbishop, but that he had refused to do so owing to the remonstrance of Bishop Bonner, who was then in the Tower ; and that, consequently, Matthew Parker and others had met together at a tavern in Cheapside, called the Nag's Head, and had proceeded to consecrate one another.    This tale was first put out in 1604—that is, forty-five years after the consecration of Matthew Parker had actually taken place—so that there was

17

little probability that any of the actual eye-witnesses
of the consecration were still living.  There did
happen to be remaining, however, one such man,
namely, the Earl of Nottingham, and he at once
denied the truth of this new story.   Moreover, it is
known that neither Pius IV., who became Pope in
the same month that Parker was made Archbishop,
nor Pius V., who issued the Bull of Deposition
against Elizabeth in 1570, ever uttered a word questioning the validity of the English Orders.   Holywood's story, however, was greedily believed, and
found a place in almost every Roman attack upon
the English Church until John Lingard, himself a
devout but honest Roman Catholic, gave it its
death-blow in his history of England which he
published in the early part of the nineteenth
century.

# CHAPTER IX

## A HOUSE DIVIDED

THE twenty-two years of the reign of James I. came to an end in 1625. With the accession of the new King, Charles I., there was at once a marked development in the growing conflict between the Sovereign and the people, for the Parliament broke with long-established usage by voting the ordinary revenue to the Crown for one year only instead of for the life of the Sovereign. This the King indignantly rejected, complaining that he had been condemned before being tried. The Parliament felt, however, that it was only by keeping tight hold on the purse-strings that it could exercise any influence at all, and it was also especially disturbed at the time by reason of the marriage of the King to Henrietta Maria, a Roman Catholic Princess of France. It seemed that constitutional and religious questions were thus inextricably bound up with one another; the

people that were fighting for liberty joined hands
with those who were opposing every appearance of
accommodation with Rome; and as each year
passed by the leaders in the Church of England
were regarded with an ever-growing suspicion.
For the first eight years of Charles's reign Archbishop Abbot lived on, and had he been able he
would have kept party feeling from becoming more
and more bitter, but the King from the very first
made him feel that he was no longer to expect that
his advice would have any weight with his Sovereign. This of itself alarmed the Puritans, but
there were other matters which disturbed them
still more. One Richard Montague, a Canon of
Windsor, and a man well known because of his
skill as a controversialist, was censured by Parliament for his High Church views and was placed
in custody. That Montague was in reality a
faithful member of the Church of England there
can be no doubt, but Parliament would have none
of him. Charles replied by making Montague one
of his chaplains. This was in 1625. A yet more
serious disagreement arose in 1627. A certain
Dr. Sibthorpe, a Northampton incumbent, had
preached a sermon asserting in the most extreme
form the doctrine of the Divine right of Kings and

the subjects' duty of passive obedience. The theory of the Divine right as now understood sounds absurd in our ears, but none of the men who upheld it at the beginning of the seventeenth century ever dreamed that it would be pushed to such lengths as it actually was afterwards. Originally it was the Protestants' defence against the Papal claim to universal sovereignty, but it was quickly made to serve against those who questioned the royal prerogative at home. Dr. Sibthorpe's sermon was, of course, denounced as soon as it was published, but again Charles showed what he thought of the matter by including the preacher amongst his chaplains. Six months later another preacher, one Roger Mainwaring, declared in the presence of the King that if the Sovereign asked for money from his subjects they were morally bound to give it. Again there were loud complaints in Parliament, and again the King showed his own mind by pardoning the preacher and presenting him to a benefice. Such teaching from the lips of the extreme Churchmen of the time welcomed as it was by the King could only result in an increase of bitterness. Such teaching also helps us to see how naturally the constitutional and the religious questions came to be merged into one. Montague had only dealt with doctrinal questions, but because his views seemed to involve an understanding with the Papacy they had a political importance.  But Sibthorpe and Mainwaring had dealt with the question of the King's prerogative ; they had said practically that men were bound to submit to their Sovereign. These preachers were not very important men ; but the King made it very clear that he approved of what they had said ; and as none of the leaders in the Church publicly disassociated themselves from such views, it was naturally believed that they were also in sympathy with them.  Discontent grew apace, but that was only a sign to Charles that there was still greater need to enforce the laws of the Church. He felt, however, that he could never do all that he desired to do so long as the Archbishopric was in the hands of one who disagreed with him on almost every point.  But that difficulty was removed when Abbot died in 1633.  Long before his death everybody had known that William Laud was to be his successor.

Laud was at this time sixty years of age.  He had been born at Reading and educated at the Free School there.  Thence he went to Oxford, and soon became a marked man by reason of his fearless opposition to the dominant Calvinism of the time. In 1611 he had been elected President of his college in spite of the opposition of Abbot and others. In 1616 he became Dean of Gloucester, and it was at Gloucester that he first showed that side of his character which was destined to cause so much trouble later on. He induced the Chapter to remove the altar of the cathedral from the nave to the chancel, but he took no pains to explain to people generally the reason for the change, and such action showed a lack of sympathy and a want of power to understand the views of others. For Laud it was enough if he knew that a thing ought to be done. His very fearlessness made him contemptuous of public opinion, and he failed to realize that no reformation, least of all a reformation in religious matters, can ever be truly brought about without the approval or at least the acquiescence of public opinion. To those who did not understand the reasons for his action the removal of the altar seemed only a tyrannical exercise of authority, and Laud had only himself to thank for such a misinterpretation of his action. Often in later years his conduct in more important matters seemed to partake of the same character. ' He did not consider enough,' wrote Clarendon in his history, ' what men said or were like to say of him.'

It was Laud's independence of character which first of all won for him the favour of King James, but later on that King valued him because he was an enthusiastic believer in the necessity for the enforcement of the Church's orders. So he had been made Bishop of S. David's in 1621. But his real influence in the national life began with the reign of Charles. He preached at the opening of the Parliaments of 1625 and 1626, and on each occasion magnified the King's authority both in Church and State. In 1628 he became Bishop of London and from that time also the King's chief adviser in all ecclesiastical matters. Laud's view was that the enforcement of outward uniformity was of the first importance because it would lead ultimately to a real unity in belief. His administration, therefore, stern and merciless as it seemed, and as, indeed, it often was, was not the tyranny of a despot who rejoiced in the mere making of his power to be felt, but rather it was the rule of the schoolmaster who would make his school efficient by the unsparing use of the rod, or of the drill-sergeant whose only thought is of the efficiency of the soldiers under him. To carry out his plans he made ready and full use of the King's support. Equally opposed to Rome and Geneva, he tried to suppress the influence of both by means of the royal authority, never apparently recognizing how dangerous such an alliance between the King and the Church might prove to be. It was natural that before long he should come to be regarded as the chief upholder of the royal tyranny ; it was equally natural that he should be regarded as favouring an understanding with Rome. On this latter point, however, he was completely misunderstood, for he recognized that the Papacy would never make any concession at all. He told Charles on one occasion that whoever wished to go to Rome would have to go all the way thither, since the Pope would take no steps to meet him.

Thus things went on for eight years from the day in 1629 when Charles got rid of his third Parliament. Then trouble arose from an unexpected quarter, and from that time it began to be seen that the only solution to the great controversies would have to be found by the sword. In 1637 an attempt was made to force upon the Scotch Church a new Prayer-Book and a new set of canons. Though Laud was not the author of either the Service Book or of the Canons, he was regarded as being responsible for them, and the great majority of Scotch people not only refused to accept them,

18

but shortly afterwards in their Parliament declared that they would not have Bishops in their Church at all. Such conduct was intolerable to Charles, and he determined to coerce his Scottish subjects. His attempt to do this, however, was not only a miserable failure so far as its immediate object was concerned, but it also compelled him to call together another English Parliament, for he was now so pressed for money that there was no other course open to him. When Parliament thus met in 1640 loud expression was given to the discontent which had been ever increasing throughout the country during the eleven years' tyranny. Puritan enthusiasts within the Church as well as constitutionalists in the State felt that at last the day of vengeance had come. The Archbishop was one of the first to be dealt with. In December, 1640, he was impeached of high treason, and in March of the following year he was sent to the Tower. There he was left until 1644, when the Commons proceeded to impeach him before the House of Lords, but finding that it would be impossible to get the Peers to convict him of treason, they resorted to a Bill of Attainder. Against this the Lords also protested for a long time, but at last, through fear of the mob, they yielded

and passed the Bill. Nothing could exceed the
dignity of Laud's conduct during these months
of his so-called trial. Again and again he protested his innocence. Though his diary and even
his Prayer-Book had been taken from him, yet
he said he was glad that he had been so treated,
for from such books, revealing as they did his
inner life, his accusers would see how true it was
that he had neither endeavoured to subvert the
laws of the kingdom nor to destroy the true
Protestant religion. No defence, however, avails a
man whose judges are also his enemies, and Laud
was executed on January 10, 1645.

But the execution of the Archbishop could not
do away with the results of his administration. By
putting him to death Parliament might express its
abhorrence of his principles, but the manner of his
death only brought those same principles the more
into prominence. His execution also helps us to
understand why the presentation in the sixteenth
century of the real position of the National Church
is associated with his name rather than with that,
for instance, of Hooker or of Andrewes. Laud
was neither so powerful a writer as Hooker nor so
truly a saint as Bishop Andrewes. But it was he
who more than any other made the position of the

English Church known to the common people. What Hooker had demonstrated the reasonableness of in a formal treatise, and what Andrewes had commended by his life to those who knew him personally, Laud enforced as the standard of Church life and teaching, using for this end the power of his office as Archbishop, and when the day of trial came he was content to die rather than yield. He had perforce to leave his work unfinished, and even when later on in 1661 the things he had aimed at received legislative sanction, a large section of the people by their secession from the Church showed that they still refused to follow his lead. But this much is certain, that from Laud's time there never was any doubt in the common mind as to what the English Church stood for.

By ordering the execution of the Archbishop Parliament made it quite clear what things it refused to sanction. It was, however, by no means equally clear what other things were to be put in their place. In June 1643 a great committee, consisting of twenty members of Parliament and four times as many ministers, and known as the ' Westminster Assembly,' was called together by Parliament, and given authority to consider the whole matter. But from the outset it was evident that there were in this committee differences as great as any that had ever divided Churchmen. The Presbyterians within it believed as emphatically as the highest Churchman that there should be one form of Church government throughout the land, and that the Church ought to be independent of all State control; the Erastians went to the opposite extreme, and said that Parliament was the Church; whilst the Independents held the view that each separate congregation was a Church in itself and entitled to manage its own affairs. Parliament naturally regarded the views of the Presbyterians with but little favour, but so long as the issue with Charles was at all doubtful and the alliance with the Scotch army therefore a matter of importance, it did not decisively reject their claims. But soon there was a stronger influence at work against Presbyterianism even than that of Parliament. This was the influence of the army under the guiding spirit of Cromwell. Parliament was mainly Erastian; the Scotch allies were Presbyterian to a man; but the army was Independent. So soon, therefore, as the common foe—the King—ceased to be of importance, the irreconcilable differences between these three parties became open and avowed, and in the end Independency as represented by the army triumphed over both its former friends, and by its triumph, though English Churchmen and Roman Catholics alike were denied liberty of worship, yet all other forms of religion were tolerated. The famous Westminster Assembly had thus failed to impose a system of Church government upon the people of England. It achieved, however, a striking success in another direction. The Confession of Faith, which was drawn up by it in 1646, became at once, and still remains, the authoritative standard of Scotch Presbyterianism, and as such has been taken by Scotchmen into every Colony of the Empire.

The long struggle with Charles ended at last in his execution. To secure this the army had expelled from the House of Commons all the members who were Presbyterian and who were therefore opposed to such a step. The remaining members, fifty-three in number, and derisively called ' The Rump,' declared that whatsoever they should resolve upon should have the force of law, and they proceeded to abolish the House of Lords as ' useless and dangerous,' and the office of King as ' useless, burdensome, and dangerous.' There followed eleven years during which the country was governed in a way which was far more unconstitu-

tional and far more out of touch with the majority
of the nation than had ever been the case in the
worst years of Charles I. During those eleven
years the Church of England was also regarded as
abolished, but it is needful to say something of the
ecclesiastical measures of that time if the reaction
which came about after the Restoration is to be
rightly understood. Before the execution of
Charles, 'The Rump' had accepted from the army
a document known as the 'Agreement of the
People,' in which it was declared that the national
religion should be 'the Christian religion reformed
to the greatest purity in doctrine, worship, and
discipline,' but yet that this national religion
should be neither Popery nor Prelacy. People
who could not conscientiously accept this new form
might have liberty to worship in their own way, but
this liberty, it was said, 'shall not necessarily extend
to Popery or Prelacy.' The liberty granted in this
Agreement was made effective in the following year,
1650, when men were set free from the obligation
of accepting the 'Solemn League and Covenant.'
Three years later 'The Rump' was ignominiously
expelled by Cromwell, and its place was taken by
an Assembly of 139 men, who had not been elected,
but who had been nominated by the Independent

ministers and their congregations throughout the country. Even this body, though so carefully chosen, found it impossible to get on with the army, and so it resigned at the end of five months. Thereupon Cromwell made it known that he would rule the country in accordance with the terms of a new document prepared by some of the army officers. In this document, known as the ' Instrument of Government,' it was at last declared definitely that neither Popery nor Prelacy should receive toleration. Moreover, in 1654 a Committee of Triers was appointed and to it was entrusted the duty of filling up vacant benefices with such persons who had ' the grace of God in them,' and who were ' able and fit to preach the Gospel.' Such appointments, however, were not to be construed as ' having the character of any solemn or sacred setting apart of a person to any particular office in the ministry.' Later on other commissioners were appointed to secure the ejection of ' scandalous ' ministers, in other words, those who still clung to the old ways, and then in the following year the unhappy men who had been thus removed were by a proclamation also debarred from acting either as schoolmasters or as domestic chaplains, or from performing any of the offices of their ministry.

Meanwhile, so little was anyone satisfied with the constitutional settlement brought about by the Instrument of Government that, after barely more than three years' experience of it, the Parliament summoned under its authority presented to Cromwell the ' Humble Petition and Advice,' in which they asked him to accept the title of King, and made other suggestions which altogether amounted to a getting back to the old form of government, only with a new dynasty, but they added a request that Popery and Prelacy might still remain forbidden. Cromwell at the desire of the army refused the title of King, but in other respects accepted the ' Petition and Advice.' Fifteen months later, however, the Protector died, and any chance this new scheme might have had of working satisfactorily died with him.

The Protector's death was succeeded by a period of unsettlement during which it became more and more evident that the only solution which would satisfy the nation generally lay in inviting the son of the executed King to take his father's place. Exactly three years after Cromwell had accepted the ' Humble Petition and Advice ' Charles landed at Dover, and began a journey to London which resolved itself into one long triumphal progress.

19

As in 1553 when the country showed its disgust with the iniquitous rule of the Protector Northumberland by tumultuously welcoming Queen Mary, so again now, a hundred years later, it spoke its mind equally clearly with regard to the despotism of the Protector Cromwell.   It was the misfortune of Cromwell that he found himself committed to a system which could not be anything but despotic. It is a question whether even he could have maintained it much longer; after he was dead scarcely anyone attempted to maintain it.

# CHAPTER X

THE return of Charles meant, of course, a return
to the old constitution. With political questions
we have here but little to do, but the settlement
arrived at in religious matters is of the greatest
importance. It must be remembered that the
King's return had been brought about not only by
the action of Churchmen, but also largely by the
influence of the Presbyterians, who hated the Independents even more than they hated Churchmen.
The hopes of this party were therefore high. They
knew they would receive toleration, for so much as
that had been promised to them as well as to others
in the declaration which the King had issued from
Breda before his return. But they trusted further
that the Liturgy of the Church might be so
amended as to enable them to conform to it. The
King favoured this idea and called together at
the Savoy twelve Bishops and twelve leading

Presbyterians to discuss the matter. The conference, however, proved a complete failure; the only
thing it could agree upon was to report to the King
that they could not agree upon any terms of comprehension; the Churchmen were but little inclined
to make concessions, for they knew that they had
the majority of the nation with them; whilst the
Presbyterians brought forward again all the old
demands which had been made at the Hampton
Court Conference in 1604. So soon as the Conference was known to be a failure, Convocation itself
appointed a committee to revise the Book of
Common Prayer. This Committee has put on
record in the preface which still stands at the forefront of the Prayer-Book the principles by which it
was guided. It rejected many of the alterations
which had been suggested to it, either because
they were 'secretly striking at some established
doctrine or laudable practice of the Church of
England, or, indeed, of the whole Catholic Church,'
or because they were 'utterly frivolous and vain;'
whilst, with regard to the alterations which it
did recommend, some, it said, were for the better
direction of the officiating clergy, some for the
purpose of removing doubts and misconstructions,
and some provided additional prayers and additional

services for special occasions.  The general effect
of the alterations was to bring out more clearly
the Catholic character of the Prayer-Book, whilst
of the additions the most notable were the
Prayer for Parliament and the Service for the
Baptism of Adults, which latter would ' be always
useful for the baptizing of the Natives in our
Plantations, and others converted to the Faith.'
The suggestions of the committee were readily
adopted by Convocation, and the use of the Prayer-
Book, as thus revised, was enforced by the Act of
Uniformity of 1662.  This compulsory use of the
Prayer-Book with its deeper note of Catholicity
would probably of itself have made it difficult for a
great many of the holders of benefices to retain
their position.  But the Act enforced other things
beside the use of the Prayer-Book : it declared that
every beneficed clergyman should be episcopally
ordained, and must renounce the Solemn League
and Covenant, and must also publicly declare that
he believed that the taking up of arms against the
King was unlawful under any pretext whatever.
The Act was thus to a large extent a political
measure, and it is not to be wondered at that a
large number of ministers—it is said nearly 2,000—
resigned rather than submit to it.  The situation

would have been hard enough if the Act had merely enforced the use of the Prayer-Book; it became impossible when it was seen that the Act demanded conformity in politics as well as in religion.   Most of those who resigned had, of course, no real legal claim to the benefices of which they were in possession; they were there in the place of the rightful occupants who had been forcibly ejected in the time of the Commonwealth; but, nevertheless, the treatment meted out to them was unnecessarily harsh.   The Act was the Act of Parliament, especially of the House of Commons, and not of the Church.   It is true that the leaders in the Church did nothing to mitigate its severity, but it is equally true that, if they had attempted to do so, they would have met with but little success, for the elections to the House of Commons which had taken place in 1661 had resulted in the return of an overwhelming majority of members who were determined to purge the Church's worship of Presbyterianism and the Church's pulpits of the politics that then commonly went with Presbyterianism.   Before it passed this Act, Parliament had already passed another, namely, the Corporation Act, which had made it impossible for any but Churchmen to hold municipal offices, and as the borough franchise was often limited to members of the Corporations, the Act indirectly said that Churchmen only should have the right to vote for members of Parliament.    Even so Parliament was not content.    Possessed with the fear that this large body of ministers who had resigned might attempt to preach another rebellion, it proceeded in 1664 to pass the Conventicle Act, which forbade any assembly for worship except such as was allowed by the Church of England ; and in the following year the Five Mile Act, which forbad all those ministers who refused to take the Oath of Non-resistance to teach in schools or to live within five miles of any corporate town.    To lessen the hardships entailed by such legislation the Lords had desired that a dispensing power should be allowed to the King, but the Commons would have none of it.    The House of Commons was, in fact, more episcopal than the Bishops and more royalist than the King.    It had already done much ; it now proceeded to do more.    It refused to forget the past or to allow others to forget it, for it ordered that January 30, the day upon which Charles I. had been put to death, should be kept as a day of fasting and humiliation, and that May 29, the day upon which Charles II.

entered London, should be kept as a day of thanksgiving.

With such emphasis did the Commons thus mark their loyalty to the King and the National Church, and it is abundantly clear that the people as a whole approved of all that they did. But before many more years had passed the same Commons had to decide which had the more weight with them, their loyalty to the King or their loyalty to the Church, and without hesitation they proceeded to defend their Church even against their King. The personal character of Charles II. is too well known to need further description. He cared for nothing except what ministered to his own selfish ends. Neither Parliament nor people were ever in love with him. He was simply welcomed at his Restoration because in his person he embodied a constitutional principle, and when as his reign went on he began to tamper with that principle, he was actively opposed. So far as he had any religious sympathies at all they were in favour of Roman Catholicism, and his real reason for desiring toleration for the Presbyterians in 1661 was that he hoped that such toleration would also be extended in due time to the Roman Catholics. The anxiety on this point which began to be felt generally throughout the country early in his reign, was seen to be only too well founded when in 1672 after the public reception of the Duke of York, the heir to the throne, into the Roman Catholic Church, the King issued a Declaration of Indulgence repealing all the legislation against Nonconformists and Roman Catholics. From that date the King lost completely the confidence of his people.  So soon as Parliament met in 1673, it compelled the King to withdraw the Declaration, and then made him accept the Test Act, by which all persons holding any office under the Crown had to take the Sacrament according to the rites of the Church of England, and to make a declaration against the doctrine of Transubstantiation.  In its next session it passed resolutions against a standing army, fearing lest such an army might be used to enforce Roman Catholicism even as it had been used a few years back under Cromwell to enforce Independency ; and in the following year the Commons went so far as to reject a Bill which would have made all office-holders declare on oath that they considered resistance against the King to be unlawful.  From this time for a period of five years the relations between the King and Parliament grew more and more strained, until finally Charles dissolved the Parliament in 1681 and

ruled for the last four years of his life without calling another.  He was able to act in this despotic
way because the opposition had at last become so
extreme that it had lost the support of public
opinion.  Their violent attempts to get the Duke
of York excluded from the succession lost them the
support of some of their followers, but the plan that
many of them were known to favour of declaring
the Duke of Monmouth, a bastard son of Charles,
the next heir, lost them still more.  So they accomplished nothing, except that they made it possible
for the King to become more despotic than his
father had ever been, and for his brother James to
remain the heir to the throne ; and people desiring
the welfare of both Church and State could only
await the future with the deepest apprehension.

Yet when in 1685 Charles died, and James was
actually in possession of the throne, it seemed that
after all these fears had been groundless, for the
new King at once stated that ' he would endeavour
to maintain the Government, both in Church and
State, as by law established,' and that ' he would
always take care to defend and support the Church
of England.'  He had, indeed, good cause to be
grateful to the National Church, for it was mainly
because it held firmly to the principle of hereditary

succession that the Bill for excluding him from the throne had never been passed. Nevertheless it was farthest from his thoughts to attempt to do anything in accordance with his promises, for he was determined to win for himself a completely despotic power. But he had set himself a task which he personally could not possibly accomplish. The thought of his brother's last four years of irresponsible rule seemed to make him forget the hostility with which he himself was regarded because of his avowed profession of Roman Catholicism. Charles through all his despotism was wise enough to leave the religion of the people alone. James imagined that he would make his despotism all the more real if he could only force his creed upon his subjects. He forgot that he had to deal with a naturally stubborn people who had most stubbornly resisted all dictation on this very point. It was this side of the King's policy which aroused the bitterest opposition and which finally brought about his downfall. For though he himself only meant his policy in religion to subserve his general aim to be despotic all round, yet the nation regarded him mainly as an agent of a hateful form of faith who was endeavouring to use his Sovereign authority to further the ends of his

master.  Only a very able man could have succeeded under such circumstances.  But James was
the reverse of able, for he was not only a narrow-
minded bigot in religious matters, but also a complete fool in statecraft.  He made the rebellions
which occurred at the opening of his reign to serve as
a pretext for increasing his standing army, and then
so ostentatiously officered that army with Roman
Catholics that people felt that an army nominally
raised to suppress unlawful rebellion might also
be used to crush constitutional opposition.  He
allowed Judge Jeffreys to deal with the rebels themselves in the ' Bloody Assizes ' in a way that made
him both hated and feared.  He removed from the
Bench the judges upon whose subserviency he could
not depend and filled their places with creatures of
his own, and then obtained from the Bench as thus
constituted a declaration that he could act in disregard of the laws of the land.  He devised a new
Ecclesiastical Court to deal with such of the clergy
as dared to oppose his policy, and by means of it
obtained the suspension of Compton, Bishop of
London, one of the most outspoken of the Bishops.
The King seemed to be possessed of an evil spirit
which was driving him on to his ruin ; many people,
indeed, said that he was mad.  And while the

nation was thus learning what Roman Catholicism in such hands might mean, Huguenot refugees were pouring into England from France bringing with them tales of the bitter sufferings which they had been made to endure at the hands of a Government which was also acting in the name of Roman Catholicism.  It came to be a question with the people not as to what the end would be, but *when* it would be.  The answer soon came.  In May 1688 James ordered that a Declaration of Indulgence in favour of Roman Catholics and Nonconformists, which had first been issued in the previous year, should now be publicly read by the clergy of the National Church in their churches during the time of Divine service.  The Archbishop of Canterbury and six Bishops thereupon presented a petition to the King in which they said that such a declaration was opposed to the law of the land, and that therefore they could not issue directions to their clergy to read it.  The King was indignant and ordered the Bishops to be committed to the Tower and to be prosecuted for having published a false and seditious libel.  The excitement in London and throughout the provinces became intense.  People who cared but little for religion felt a new regard for Bishops who dared to fight for national liberty ; while Nonconformists who in their own way cared much for religion and yet were made to suffer under the existing laws, with splendid self-forgetfulness were amongst their most enthusiastic supporters.   Then, in the midst of all this excitement and whilst the Bishops were still waiting their trial, came the news that a son had been born to the King !  Nobody believed the truth because nobody wanted to believe it.   They had, it must be said, some ground for their incredulity.   The King had lost his first wife seventeen years before, and had been married to his second wife for fifteen years, and up to this time she had borne him no children.   It was the fact that the King had had no son which had given the nation a kind of patience.   It knew that on the death of James his successor would be his daughter Mary, who was a devout member of the English Church and whose husband was William of Orange, the Protestant ruler of Holland.   Such a prospect was destroyed by the birth of the son, and the common people in the bitterness of their disappointment declared that the child was supposititious.   Of more consequence however was the influence that this event had upon the great men in Church and State.   They, dreading that a Roman Catholic son might continue the policy of his

Roman Catholic father, invited William of Orange to come over and help them in their struggle for their constitutional liberties. On September 30, 1668 William answered that he would accede to their request. But James feared to await the issue of events. Three months earlier the exuberant joy with which the acquittal of the seven Bishops had been received had taught him something of the state of public opinion. Now two days before the Christmas of that year he fled to France, and after much debating in and out of Parliament it was declared that James had by his flight abdicated the throne, and the crown was then settled upon William and Mary.

# CHAPTER XI

WITH the flight of James and the accession of William and Mary the political crisis was practically at an end. It was far different, however, with regard to ecclesiastical affairs. With the coming of William a new chapter opens in the history of the English Church. The Church, by the bold front which it had presented to the late King, had in reality made the Revolution possible, but so soon as the Revolution was over it was seen that it, at least, would suffer rather than gain under the new order. This was due to two causes. In the first place, William III. had no love for the Church. He had been reared as a Presbyterian, and had grown up a Latitudinarian. Moreover, he had only one object in life, namely, the destruction of the power of Louis XIV. of France. To the accomplishment of that object he directed all his energies and enlisted aid from every possible source. Hence he regarded England merely as part of a great European coalition, and in order to give that coalition an additional strength he wished so to Protestantize the English Church that it might come into line with the Protestant forces on the Continent, and thus make the war against Louis a war of Protestantism *versus* Roman Catholicism as well as a war against the overweening ambition of the French King.   He would use religious animosity to crush a political rival.

The other cause was that the ablest and truest Churchmen of the time were just those who felt themselves unable to take the new oaths of allegiance to William and Mary.   James II. was still their King, and his subjects, so they believed, had no power to depose him.   His conduct indeed compelled his subjects to regard him as insane, and therefore he could not be suffered to exercise the authority of a King ; a Regency must be appointed to act in his name for the rest of his life.   William and the Whig politicians who supported him might have ignored these views inasmuch as James was in exile and William and Mary were actually upon the throne, but, instead of doing so, they made the taking of the new oaths compulsory. William, at any rate, looked forward with some-

thing more than complacency to the possibility of
many of the greater Churchmen refusing to take
these oaths, for if they refused to do so they would
be deprived of their offices, and their place would
at once be filled with men who could be trusted
to bring the English Church into harmony with
Protestantism abroad.   When the oaths were ten-
dered about 400 clergy refused to take them, at
their head being Archbishop Sancroft himself and
three of the other Bishops who had formed the
famous seven.   It was a cruel fate that some of
those who had played so great a part in the vindication of national liberty should be thus amongst the
first to suffer under the new King.   But it is of
more consequence to note that the effect upon the
Church was disastrous.   Not only was it deprived
of its strongest men, but it began to be officered by
others who were not merely out of sympathy with
its general teaching, but were further pledged to
alter that teaching in its essential features.   The
worst aspects of the government of Edward VI.
were revived : the National Church was to be used
for political purposes, and this end was to be arrived
at by the careful filling of its prominent posts with
men who could be trusted to make the aims of the
Government their chief concern.   This policy was

continued with but little intermission by one
Government after another for nearly three-quarters
of a century.   William adopted it in order, as we
have seen, to make the alliance between England
and the Protestant Powers as close a one as possible.
But when the Hanoverian line of Sovereigns began
in 1714 there seemed to the politicians of those
days a greater reason still why the filling up of
vacancies in the Church should be regarded as of
great political importance.   For it was common
knowledge that no one welcomed the Hanoverians,
and that they were only accepted as a disagreeable
necessity : they were foreigners in their habits as well
as in their speech: there was nothing about them
to attract the loyalty of the people : ' the divinity
that doth hedge a King ' seemed gone for ever.
Yet every effort had to be made to keep George I.,
and then George II., upon the throne, for the only
alternative was to accept once again the line of the
Stuarts.   So the pulpits were ' tuned ' again ; promotion was to be the reward for faithful political
service ; enthusiasm was to be discouraged relentlessly lest it might lead to Jacobitism ; the election
to bishoprics was to become a farce ; and the
Bishops instead of being shepherds of the flock
were to become Government agents, representing

a policy which no one liked but which many hated. The full consequences of this policy will be seen later on. During William's reign they were dreaded rather than felt. In the place of Sancroft the King chose John Tillotson, a man justly esteemed for the character of his private life, but a Puritan by birth and training, and quite ready to carry out, if possible, the King's plans. More significant still, as indicating the new policy, was the appointment of Gilbert Burnet to the See of Salisbury. Burnet was a Scotchman who had spent much time at The Hague in the Court of the Prince of Orange, and who had there taken a very active part in promoting William's expedition to England. William, therefore, owed him a great deal for his political services, but he valued him also because of his Low Church views. Yet the very considerations which made him acceptable to William made him equally disliked by the clergy of his diocese. It is due to his memory to say that he took up his work as Bishop with rare zeal and devotion, treating with equal courtesy enemies and friends, and labouring in every way to approve himself to his flock, but nothing really availed him as against his hated political opinions. After his appointment as

Bishop he still continued to be one of the King's most intimate counsellors. It was on his advice that Tillotson was chosen to succeed Sancroft and that Tenison was appointed Bishop of Lincoln; and, further, that when Tillotson died in 1694 Tenison succeeded to the Archbishopric, Burnet recommending him not because he was the best man available, but because it was felt that the arduous task of quieting the discontented and distracted Church could most safely be entrusted to him.

The great constitutional crisis of 1688 had been produced, as we have seen, by the attempt of James II. to introduce Roman Catholicism. In that struggle the main body of Nonconformists had been staunch allies of the National Church, and this co-operation in the pursuit of a common end had brought about amongst both Churchpeople and Dissenters a real regard for one another and a true respect for each other's convictions. This better understanding produced the Toleration Act of 1689—an Act which also marks the beginning of a new epoch in the ecclesiastical history of England. The Act was by no means a complete measure, for it did not grant liberty of worship to Roman Catholics nor to any body of Dissenters which did not hold the Trinitarian Faith.  Neither did it do away with the civil disabilities which were attached to Dissent, for the Nonconformist as such was still unable to become a member of a Borough Corporation or to sit as a member of Parliament. Yet, nevertheless, the Act is of great importance, because it embodied a new principle.  For the previous century and a half, ever since the time, indeed, when the Reformation changes had begun to be made, every party in the State had striven for uniformity in worship throughout the land. Henry VIII. in his legislation, the foreign Protestant party under Edward VI., the Papalists of Mary's time, the statesmen of Elizabeth, the Laudian Bishops, the Puritan forces of the Commonwealth, and the Cavalier Parliament, had each and all aimed at enforcing their own ideals upon the whole community.  The Toleration Act was at last a public confession that uniformity had become an impossibility, and that nothing better could be done than to legalize diversity.

It is recognized now that that was the only possible solution of the matter, but the people of the seventeenth century were slow to see it, and many of them only accepted it with reluctance when it came.  From the point of view of the

Church itself, the Act was a proof of failure as well as a mark of success. Henceforth the theological position of the Church which men like Hooker and Andrewes and Laud had each in his own way constantly upheld becomes its recognized position. So far the Church had triumphed. But the triumph was acquiesced in by those who did not accept the Church's teaching because they themselves were now to be allowed to live their religious life apart from it.

William signed the Act with real willingness, though it did not express his own views. He was one of those who still hoped that uniformity might be secured. But this uniformity which he desired was, as we have seen, of the kind that would have reduced the Church to the level of the foreign Protestant sects. In accordance with his wishes a Comprehension Bill was introduced into the House of Lords and passed by that body. The Bill met with a very different fate, however, at the hands of the Commons. They said that nothing of the kind could be considered by them unless it came to them with the consent of the Convocations of the Church. William was much annoyed at this statement, but found himself obliged to acquiesce. Convocation was summoned, and a committee was

appointed to prepare a scheme of such alterations
in the Prayer-Book as would satisfy the Dissenters
and enable them to come within the Church again.
The scheme was prepared and duly presented, but
its failure was certain long before it was submitted,
for it had become known that the suggestions
amounted to a complete revolution in the Church's
worship.   Burnet, though willing to accept the
proposed changes, at once realized that they would
never be adopted.   Everybody, he said, declared
that the Church was to be pulled down and
Presbytery be set up.  Conscientious Churchmen
had indeed good cause for complaint.  They had
accepted the Toleration Act, and by it had
admitted that those who did not like their methods
of worship might freely adopt some other; but
now they were to be further asked to give up their
own ways.   They felt that at least the Toleration
which had recently been extended to the Dissenters
might be granted to them also.  Toleration and
Comprehension expressed indeed exactly opposite
ideas.   If Toleration were right, then attempts to
enforce Comprehension upon unwilling subjects
must be wrong; whilst if Comprehension was
ideally right, then the Toleration Act ought never
to have been passed.  On every ground this

attempt on the part of William to Protestantize the Church was foredoomed to failure. As a matter of fact, so definite was the opposition to it that it was never actually discussed in Convocation at all.

The Dutch King never strove to secure by personal influence what he had failed to secure by means of Parliament. His reign marks the definite recognition of the fact that in political affairs the sovereign power had passed in reality, if not in form, out of the hands of the King into the hands of Parliament, and there were many people ready to assert that the like authority in ecclesiastical affairs had similarly passed to Parliament. We are tempted to forget the importance of the Revolution of 1688, because it was accomplished without bloodshed; there was neither a Naseby, nor a beheadal at Whitehall; yet in reality the Revolution which put William and Mary on the throne was the beginning of modern England. From that time the supremacy of Parliament in political affairs has been unquestioned, except for the twenty years when George III. tried to govern in the old autocratic way. From that time also it is claimed that the power of the King in ecclesiastical matters has also passed to Parliament.

22

That the interests of the Church might be seriously affected by this change was seen when the House of Lords was quite prepared to pass a Comprehension Bill without any reference to the wishes of the Church at all. No harm was done then, however, for the House of Commons acknowledged the right of the Church to deal with such things in the first instance. Moreover, the members of both Houses of Parliament at that time were of necessity Churchmen. Since then the doors of Parliament have been thrown open to all sorts and conditions of men, and it has long been a serious question whether Parliament so constituted ought to exercise the ecclesiastical jurisdiction which had originally been vested in the King himself.

With the passing of the Toleration Act, and the consequent cessation of internal strife, there came a marked development in the proper work of the National Church in two directions, one a revival of the work it had nobly done in an earlier day, the other a new work imposed upon it by the circumstances of the time: these were the education of the people and the evangelization of the heathen.

The spoliation of the Church in the sixteenth

century had grievously affected its educational work. The monastic schools, which had existed in every country district, had never been replaced, for those who had confiscated the Church's property had done nothing more than build some few Grammar Schools in the more considerable market-towns, whilst the civil strife of the middle of the seventeenth century had effectually prevented any real educational progress. At the close of the century the general ignorance was indeed appalling. The father of John Wesley, for example, said that in his great parish not one in twenty knew the Lord's Prayer, and fewer still the Belief, and what was true of his parish was true of the country as a whole. It was in part to remedy such a state of things that the first of the great Church societies was started—the Society for Promoting Christian Knowledge. In May 1688 a devout clergyman, named Thomas Bray, got together four communicant laymen, and with them agreed to meet and consult as often as convenient under, as they said, 'the conduct of Divine Providence and assistance,' to promote Christian knowledge. The Society, in spite of opposition, grew with great rapidity. By means of it charity schools were started for the clothing,

feeding, and educating of poor children, and so
great was the influence of the new movement that
within five years there were fifty such schools in
or near London. Schools for illiterate adults were
also begun, and then in order that the people when
taught should have wholesome literature to read,
cheap and good books were printed for distribution
broadcast. This was the beginning of all modern
elementary educational work, and for more than a
century the whole burden of such elementary
education as was being given at all was borne by
this Society.

Not less important was the attempt that was
made by the same notable group of five Churchmen
to provide for the spiritual needs of English
settlers abroad, and for the conversion of the
natives who dwelt within 'the Plantations.' Up
to this time English people had been as a rule
sadly indifferent to the importance of foreign
missionary work, although amongst the schemes
of Archbishop Laud was one for the creation of
Bishoprics in North America. The neglect of the
English Church in this direction is in striking
contrast to the zeal of the Roman Catholics.
Before the end of the sixteenth century the
Jesuits had developed a regular missionary system,

and in 1622 the care and direction of the Roman
missionaries was taken over by the College of
Cardinals at Rome, and from that time the
missions have been part of the foreign policy of
the Roman Church, and have received the support
and invigoration which comes from the knowledge
that they thus represent their Church abroad.
Such a statesmanlike attempt to deal with a vast
undertaking appealed to the imagination of Oliver
Cromwell, and he desired to establish a committee
which should in like manner take charge of
Protestant missionary effort, but the religious
difficulties which then divided English people
prevented any really representative effort of this
kind being made.    By an Order in Council issued
by Charles I. all British subjects abroad had been
placed under the care of the Bishop of London,
and in 1685 a certain Dr. Blair had been sent as a
Commissary to Virginia.    But no real attempt to
deal with the problem took place until Dr. Bray
was sent as Commissary to Maryland in 1699.
The society which Dr. Bray and his faithful friends
had then recently started had included in its
objects the provision of missionaries for the Plantations, and the good man had now an opportunity
of finding out for himself the real needs of the

Colonies. Before very long he was back again in England, and so inspired Archbishop Tenison and the Bishop of London with his enthusiasm that they secured from William III. Letters Patent under the Great Seal creating a corporation by the name of the Society for the Propagation of the Gospel in Foreign Parts, which should take in hand the foreign work of the Church. This was in 1701—that is, little more than two years after Dr. Bray first took counsel with his friends as to what could be done for the cause of Christ both at home and abroad. In such ways this faithful priest, supported by four equally faithful laymen, with a complete absence of ostentation and with but little assistance originally from high quarters, began the modern work of the National Church. They rightly occupy a high place in the regard of all English Churchpeople. But they also illustrate how almost completely the Episcopate at the end of the seventeenth century was indifferent to, or at least ignorant of, the needs of the time. Efforts which the Bishops ought to have originated and guided were left by them to be undertaken by the rank and file, and the result has not been without harm, since these activities, which ought to have been made from the very first the official

concern of the whole English Church, came to be
regarded at the best as but laudable objects which
individual members of the Church might support
if they wished so to do.   They were left to the
enthusiasm of the few, and even still are too
seldom regarded as the work of the whole Church.

William III., 'the Dutch King' as he was called
by some, 'the Usurper' as he was called by not a
few, died in 1702.   If he was but little regarded
by the mass of Churchpeople he had only himself
to thank.   He was succeeded by his wife's sister,
the Princess Anne, and with the new sovereign
there came a great change in the ecclesiastical
policy, for whilst William had been a Calvinist,
Anne had always been a devout believer in the
traditional position of the English Church.   Yet
the change scarcely made for the real good of the
Church, for it only meant that the Royal Patronage
was now given to the High Church party instead
of, as formerly, to the Latitudinarians ; and the
High Churchmen of those days were just as eager
as their opponents to use the Royal influence to
further their own ends.   Party spirit had never
been at rest ; it was now enormously increased by
the bitterness of those on the one hand who,
having been for ten or twelve years supreme, were

now in adversity; and on the other hand by the unconcealed exultation of those who were now basking in the Royal favour. The extent of this factious spirit is seen in the famous trial of Dr. Sacheverell in 1710. Sacheverell, who was little better than a clerical wind-bag, had preached two sermons roundly denouncing the Whigs both in politics and in the Church, who were according to him ' conformists in faction, half conformists in practice, and non-conformists in judgment.' It was the party spirit which produced the sermons; it was the same spirit which made the House of Commons take notice of them and impeach the preacher; and it was the same spirit which made the Tories in politics and the High Churchmen in the Church rejoice at the practical acquittal of the offender. The trial, as a matter of fact, is only worthy of remembrance at all because it produced a great political reaction throughout the country, so that in the autumn of 1710, when a new Parliament was elected, it was found to be over-whelmingly Tory, and this Tory Government proceeded to pass violent reactionary measures embodying the views of the narrowest of the High Churchmen. Nonconformists, excluded by earlier legislation from municipal life, had been for some years accustomed to occasional conformity so as to attain their ends. This was now distinctly forbidden, and any infringement of the law was to be visited by heavy penalties. Soon after came also the 'Schism Act,' which forbade any Nonconformist from keeping a school or acting as a tutor. The effect of both measures was of course only to increase in the minds of Dissenters a dislike of the Church.

But the party spirit of the time found its fullest expression within the walls of Convocation. During the greater part of William's reign this body had not been allowed to meet at all; and when it was summoned in 1701, it was seen at once that, owing to the political character of the King's appointments, there was a wide divergence of views between the Upper House and the Lower. This produced during the reign of Queen Anne an unceasing and oftentimes an unseemly strife between the houses as to their relative rights and powers.

The Church was suffering grievously because its fortunes for the time being were in the hands of men who were only party leaders. This was almost entirely true of the Bishops, and was also largely the case with regard to the parochial clergy. For the noblest spirits of the time were to be found among the Non-Jurors, the people who had refused to take the oaths of allegiance to William and Mary, and thus, because of their attitude in political affairs, were living in a forced isolation and unable to have any influence over the course of events.  In their ranks were to be found such men as Francis Cherry of Shottesbrooke, in Berkshire, a pattern of what an English country gentleman should be ; Henry Dodwell, the Camden Professor of History at Oxford until he was deprived in 1691, whose learning received the praise of Gibbon, and whose character made Addison speak of him as a parson in a 'tye-wig'; Robert Nelson, the author of the 'Companion for the Festivals and Fasts of the Church of England,' a work which had deservedly a wide popularity, and who, beside his literary labours, promoted the founding of theological colleges, hospitals for incurables, and ragged, or as he called them, 'blackguard schools'; and amongst the clergy John Kettlewell of Coleshill, who was deprived in 1690, 'a perfect pattern of quiet Christian devotion and of unfailing charity'; and Anthony Horneck, preacher at the Savoy, 'of unsullied purity and unfailing courtesy.'  But the most famous of all the Non-Jurors was Thomas

Ken, Bishop of Bath and Wells, who was deprived in 1691, but who felt so keenly the evil of schism that in 1701 he suggested to Bishop Lloyd of Norwich, the only other remaining Non-Juror Bishop, that they should both resign, and thus make it impossible for anyone to question the jurisdiction of the men who had been placed in their sees. This good Bishop has secured for himself a more certain fame, however, by reason of his devotional poetry. For the third edition of his ' Manual of Prayers for Winchester College' he composed the hymns ' Awake, my soul, and with the sun,' and ' Glory to Thee, my God, this night'—hymns which are now sung wherever there is an English congregation. His declaration of faith, as expressed in his will, is also worthy of record. He died, he said, in the Communion of the Church as it stands distinguished from all Papal and Puritan innovations. With his death the Non-Jurors as a party may be said to have ceased to exist, but the unhappy condition of the Church at that time is the best proof of how much the influence of these holy men had been needed.

Queen Anne died in 1714, and, in pursuance of the terms of the Act of Settlement passed thirteen years before, she was succeeded by George of

Hanover. This arrangement had been made so as to secure the exclusion of the son of James II., but it meant further difficulties for that great body of Churchpeople who were committed to the doctrine of hereditary succession. To destroy as far as possible within the Church every antagonistic influence to the new order of things became at once the prime concern of the Government of the new King, and in the hands of Walpole, his chief Minister, this work was only too effectually done. The Church was too powerful either to be ignored or to be opposed; it was necessary, therefore, to inoculate it. The bishoprics, as they fell vacant, were filled by the supporters of the Hanoverians, and by them only. The regard of such men for their pastoral office was of the lowest; enthusiasm they had none; zeal for the salvation of souls they scarcely understood; their best efforts were directed only towards the intellectual defence of the Christian Faith, but such work, however convincing it might be to the mind, never stirred the heart. And in course of time, as opportunities arose for the exercise of the patronage which belonged to their sees, many of the rectories and vicarages in their dioceses came to be filled with men like themselves. There was much discontent at first at this condition of things, but that discontent was unable to find articulate expression, for Walpole, with a sinister insight, had quietly suppressed Convocation. The opportunity for doing this had arisen in 1717 when the Lower House was openly and violently challenging the opinions of one Benjamin Hoadly, a man who had recently become Bishop of Bangor. Hoadly had long been known as a strong opponent of the Non-Jurors, and there was little doubt that with the coming of the Hanoverians he would receive high preferment. This anticipation was fulfilled almost at once, for within a year of the accession of King George he received the offer of the bishopric ; and he signalized his promotion by writing a clever attack upon the Non-Jurors and also by preaching before the King a sermon in which he denied the existence of any visible Church of God upon earth. The book was sufficiently provocative, but the sermon, challenging as it did the opinions of a far larger number of people, aroused widespread resentment, and that resentment developed into bitter denunciation when it was known that the sermon was to be published by the royal command. So intense was the feeling that as many as seventy-four pamphlets dealing with the questions at issue were published in one month alone. The excitement among Church-people generally was reflected in the Lower House of Convocation where the Bishop's opinions were condemned without a single voice being raised in their support, and the Upper House was thereupon requested to deal with the matter. It was at this moment that the Government of the King, becoming alarmed at the force of the attack which was being made upon one of its chief supporters, prorogued Convocation and thus stifled public discussion. Such a policy, when once adopted, was found to be too convenient to be easily dropped ; moreover, the irritation which was in existence in 1717 was certainly not less real in 1718 after an enforced silence of twelve months. So Convocation after meeting for formal business was immediately prorogued again, and this course was adopted on every succeeding occasion for 132 years. For some time it was said that the Church could not be trusted to express its voice in its own constitutional assembly lest the welfare of the Hanoverian succession should become endangered. Afterwards, when the deadening influence of the principles of the Hanoverian Bishops had produced its effect, the Church itself grew indifferent, and was content to keep within its mouth the gag which had originally been placed there by its falsest of friends.   The wonder is that dead as the Church was at the end of the eighteenth century it was not then more dead still.   During that century when questions of the gravest importance were pressing for settlement, when a wise handling of the movement started by the Wesleys needed to be devised, when the shifting of the population from the countryside to the towns was causing serious anxiety, when the Churchmen of the United States were asking for Bishops from the Motherland from which they had just revolted— during all that time the mind of the Church as a whole never found expression in Convocation, and individual Bishops managed or mismanaged affairs each in his own diocese or let them alone to take their own course.   The memory of such a time will surely never cease to bring with it a feeling of deep shame—a feeling which is only made somewhat less bitter when it is remembered that this paralysis in Church life was not wholly due to the Church itself, but was rather produced by the action of a political party driven thereto by the consciousness of the fact that they were in power in spite of the views of the majority of the people.

The Bangorian Controversy, as the quarrel over

Bishop Hoadly's views was called, produced another result besides that of the suppression of Convocation. It led to the widespread dissemination of the opinions which the Bishop represented, for the people who ridiculed the idea of the Divine authority of the Church found in those views what seemed to them to be a logical basis for their position. So it came about that amongst the clergy generally the Laudian teaching which had been the common characteristic at the end of the seventeenth century, was scarcely heard at all at the end of the eighteenth, and this change found practical expression in various ways: the Rubrics of the Prayer-Book were disregarded everywhere and on all occasions ; the Sacraments of the Church were less esteemed and therefore less frequently celebrated ; and both the Bishops and the clergy, regarding their pastoral office lightly, found that their people came to regard it lightly also.

# CHAPTER XII

## THE METHODISTS

W HILST such a change was taking place within the
Church a change was occurring also in the social
condition of England which had had no parallel in
all the previous history of the country.  This change
was twofold : the population began to increase,
at first twice as quickly and later on three or even
four times as quickly as ever it had done before ;
and also the increased numbers, instead of being
evenly distributed over the country as a whole,
were found to be gathering together around a
comparatively few centres.  There is no need here
to give any detailed account of the cause of this
change.  Briefly, it may be said that it came about
partly through improvements in means of com-
munication, but chiefly through Watt's invention
of the steam-engine, which in turn led to the intro-
duction of the factory system.  The erection of
factories meant the massing together of the people

who worked in them, the people who hitherto
had lived in cottage homes in different villages.
Furthermore, since the steam-engine consumed an
immense quantity of coal, the factories became also
to a large extent grouped together in comparatively
small areas in the Centre and North of England
where the coal could be most cheaply obtained.
These changes led to an enormous increase in
the money wealth of the country, but for a
long time they involved also a very serious loss
of well-being to the mass of the people. The
conditions of life under which the workers lived
in these new districts were as unsatisfactory as
possible. People were herded together in new-
made towns hideous in their ugliness and lacking
even a pretence at sanitation; the old personal
relation between master and man disappeared, for
the workpeople were henceforth only so many
' hands,' regarded by the capitalists merely as so
many necessary instruments in the production of
the goods out of which they made their immense
fortunes. Circumstances so brutal naturally brutal-
ized the people, until it came to pass that in many
a case sin almost ceased to be sin because the
transgressor knew not that he was transgressing.
Never had there been greater need for the Church's

ministrations ; never a greater need for a ministry which would faithfully proclaim before all men the teaching of Christ, and which would especially remind the rich men of the responsibility which goes with the possession of wealth. Yet the National Church did next to nothing. In these new manufacturing districts many a village suddenly became a town, and such of the parish clergy as troubled themselves about the matter at all found themselves face to face with social problems which their previous experience had given them absolutely no capacity to deal with, nor as to which could they expect to receive any help from their Bishops. There was no discussion about these serious matters in Convocation since, as we know, Convocation was practically non-existent, and there was no strengthening of the hands of the clergy by the laity, for the laymen were as indifferent as were their parish priests. At last, however, a change did come, but when it came it seemed as though the National Church could only give further proof of the depth to which it had sunk. For though the new life had its origin within her womb, she herself not only did nothing to foster its growth, but she would willingly at one time have taken a part in putting it to death.

Towards the close of the seventeenth century the moral degradation in the national life for which the Court of Charles II. was almost entirely responsible had so distressed the better men in the kingdom that efforts had been made by them to create a counteracting influence, and parochial associations, known as Religious Societies, had therefore been formed in many places for the deepening of the spiritual life of their members.  Attendance at Holy Communion and the observance of the Fasts and Vigils ordered by the Prayer-Book had always first place in their rules; but reality in their private devotional life was equally insisted upon ; and special preachers who would encourage such ideals became in great request.  The movement rapidly grew to be an important one though the Bishops generally, and especially such of them as owed their promotion to William III., did their best to discourage it.  One of these Societies was destined to be productive of an especially great result.  A country clergyman named Samuel Wesley, Rector of Epworth in Lincolnshire, had formed a Religious Society in his parish on the eve of the Festival of the Purification, 1702, and by means of it had done much to raise the standard of Churchmanship amongst his people.  Of this good Rector's nineteen children one was the John Wesley who later on played so wonderful a part in the revival of religion in England. This son John, after being educated at the Charterhouse and at Oxford, became ordained and acted for a short while as his father's curate. He then went back to Oxford and found that his brother Charles, who was still in residence, had started a Religious Society like the one with which both the young men were familiar at Epworth. He at once became a member of it and by reason of his stronger personality became also its leader. Encouraged by glad words of commendation from their father, the brothers went on their way and before long were joined by many of their University friends. One of these friends was George Whitefield, at that time a poor student of Pembroke College, who as a lad had acted as drawer of the beer for the customers of the little public-house kept by his mother at Gloucester, but who later on was destined to become almost as famous as Wesley himself. As the Society grew it attracted the notice of the University generally and, like all such new movements, it had to face the derision and contempt both of those who despised it and of those who though approving of it in their conscience were yet too weak to dare to join it.

Out of the many nicknames given to it, one, namely that of ' Methodists,' survived, and has remained as the general title of the different divisions into which the followers of the Wesleys and Whitefield have since grouped themselves. This name was given to the first members of the movement because of their careful observance of the directions contained in the Prayer-Book, and it bears eloquent testimony to their fidelity in a careless age to the teaching of the Church of which they were members.

Five years after the formation of the Society in Oxford John Wesley went as a missionary under the auspices of the Society for the Propagation of the Gospel to the newly formed colony of Georgia in America, and, during his absence, Whitefield by his remarkable eloquence made the new movement known to everyone, both in the West of England and in London. But success also meant opposition. Many people had no desire to be aroused out of their spiritual lethargy; some saw in the new enthusiasm dangers both to Church and State; many of the clergy were angry at what they regarded as an intrusion into spheres which they said rightly belonged to themselves alone; many others of them decried the movement because it only too plainly revealed their own lack of spiritual earnestness; whilst not a few saw the seeds of a fresh schism in the Religious Societies which were springing up everywhere.  Here was a movement new in its enthusiasm and to many new in its methods.  In spite of opposition it was spreading every day by reason of the extraordinary devotion and fervour of its leaders.  But unfortunately there was no one in authority who knew how to control it so as to make it a force to awaken a slumbering Church.  On the great question as to whether there was room within the Church for the Religious Societies Wesley consulted the Bishop of London of the time.  ' Are they dissenting conventicles ?' he said.  ' I think not,' replied the Bishop, ' but I determine nothing ; read the Acts and laws on the subject for yourselves.'  What a reply from the chief pastor of a diocese in which these Societies already abounded !  The great Bishop Butler of Bristol was more definite, but it was the definiteness of opposition.  He said to Wesley : ' You have no business here ; you are not commissioned to preach in this diocese ; therefore I advise you to go hence.'  From that moment the issue could not much longer remain in doubt.  In 1739, within a year of Wesley's interview with the

Bishop of London, he formed a Society under his own control in London, and the Wesleyan movement as a movement distinct from the life of the National Church was begun. Of the subsequent history of that movement we have nothing to do here. It need only be said that, when it had finally developed into religious organizations definitely separated from the Church, it was found that the Church had lost very many of its best children, since the ranks of Methodism were recruited mainly from the trading classes and shopkeepers and the better class of artisans and labourers—that is, from those classes which make up so largely the backbone of England.

# CHAPTER XIII

## NEW LIFE WITHIN THE CHURCH

SEPARATION was not, however, the only result of the movement which originated with the Wesleys at Oxford. Many of the men who very early came under the influence of that movement were content to remain true to their Church and to labour on within it in the belief that it would once again justify its position as the Church of the nation. To their influence was due the revival within the Church which is known as the Evangelical Movement. Their object was the same as that of the Wesleys and Whitefield: they laboured to convince the world of the awfulness of sin, and to make each man realize his own personal responsibility before God; but they laboured within and not without the Church.

Of these men, perhaps the noblest was John William Fletcher, for many years Vicar of Madeley in Shropshire. Fletcher was of Swiss origin (his

name really was De la Flechere), but he made
England his home.  While he acted with Wesley
he did much by preaching to French-speaking
people in London ; and so great a regard had
Wesley for him that when in 1773 it seemed likely
that he, Wesley, would die, he hoped that the
leadership of the revival would be undertaken by
his friend.  But it was as Vicar of his large country
parish that Fletcher did his best work.  The in-
difference of his people to all holy things formed
only an additional incentive to him to devote his
energies to their welfare.  He even adopted the
method of going round the parish at 5 a.m. on
Sunday mornings with a bell in order to rouse the
people and call them to worship.  He was also an
enthusiastic believer in what was then the new
system of Sunday-schools.  His personal holiness
moreover was as remarkable as his zeal, so that his
visits to the new Theological College at Trevecca
were regarded as the visits of an angel of God,
while a man who called to see him when he was old
and infirm said : ' I was told I should see a man
with one foot in the grave, but I found a man that
had one foot in heaven.'

Another of the leaders was John Newton, a man
who in his early years had been a wild and disso-

lute sailor, but later had come under the influence
of Whitefield at Liverpool. After that he was
ordained, and did excellent work as curate-in-
charge of Olney in Buckinghamshire. But it was
as a writer of spiritual letters that men knew
him best, though now, like Bishop Ken, he is
remembered as a hymn-writer; and two at least of
his hymns, ' How sweet the name of Jesus sounds,'
and 'Glorious things of Thee are spoken,' are
amongst the most loved in the English language.

A third man was Henry Venn, who, as Vicar of
Huddersfield for twelve years, was able to make
the Christian Faith a real influence in one of the
new manufacturing towns of his time, and, later
on, as incumbent of Yelling in Huntingdonshire,
became spiritual adviser to many a Cambridge
student.

By the influence of men of this kind there was a
new life springing up within the National Church
in many parts of the country. But the centre of
the movement was quickly recognized as being at
Clapham, a place which was then little more than
a village lying close to London. John Venn, a son
of the Vicar of Huddersfield, was Rector of
Clapham from 1792 to 1813, and amongst his
parishioners were included some of the noblest

laymen of the time. One of these was Henry Thornton, a distinguished city merchant, well-known alike for his integrity and for his munificence. Others were Zachary Macaulay, the father of the historian, and Mr. James Stephen. But far and away the most distinguished of a very notable group was William Wilberforce, a member of an old Yorkshire family, who had begun his public life merely as a popular member of Parliament, but who later on became one of the most enthusiastic members of what was already known as 'the Clapham sect.' It is because the Evangelical Movement possessed in this one centre such a number of truly remarkable men that it was able to become so effective for good. Each of these men had they lived apart would have done much; living together they did perhaps a greater work than any similar body of men has ever yet done. It was not merely that the strength of the centre gave constant encouragement to individual members throughout the land, though that was much. Besides this the 'Claphamites' inaugurated at least two great movements, and gave such support to a third as to make it finally successful. They started a new Missionary Society which should supplement the work of the Society for the Propagation of the Gospel in Foreign Parts by sending men to Africa and the East. After a few years this Society received the name of the Church Missionary Society, and soon became what it still honourably remains—viz., the most enthusiastic of all the societies engaged in the work of the evangelization of the heathen races. Subsequently the same men started also the British and Foreign Bible Society in order that copies of the Scriptures might be furnished in abundance to all who desired them, and the work of this Society in publishing translations of the Scriptures in practically every known tongue has been of inestimable value to Nonconformist and American Foreign Missions as well as to the Church's own missionaries.

But the cause into which these men threw more energy still was that for the abolition of the Slave Trade. Such a cause found in William Wilberforce a leader, who, by his position in Parliament, by his known friendship with Pitt, and by his general popularity, could have done much for any object, but who, just because he was filled with a deep religious enthusiasm and was whole-heartedly supported by friends who shared his views, was even able at last to persuade Parliament to put a stop to the Slave Trade. This triumph was achieved in 1807, and though slavery as a recognized institution within the Empire did not come to an end until the great Emancipation Act of 1833, yet it was felt from the first that that would follow. In addition also to their efforts to suppress this terrible traffic the Evangelicals founded the colony of Sierra Leone in the hope that it would prove the centre of new influences for the improvement of the social condition of the native races in Africa, an attempt which was none the less noble because it proved ultimately unsuccessful. In fact, every project of the time which seemed to be designed for the good of men at home or abroad, either owed its origin to the " Claphamites " themselves or was sure of their hearty support.

Nevertheless this Evangelical Movement did not retain its commanding position within the National Church after the death of its first leaders. It had arisen in an age which was strongly individualistic, and it partook of the character of its time ; the movement was the work of a collection of individuals and not of a corporate body. It was also narrow in its sympathies, refusing to have any part in much of the life and recreation of the nation, and this in spite of the broader and more genial spirit of William Wilberforce. Furthermore, its mem-

bers made little of the Sacraments of the Church ;
they met for Prayer - Meetings rather than for
worship and listened to sermons instead of par-
taking of the Holy Communion. It was the Puritan
attitude of the time of Queen Elizabeth over again,
with this addition that the Puritans at the beginning of the nineteenth century were honourably
distinguished by their good works.

Meanwhile, there were great changes at work in
the minds of the people generally. The French
Revolution actually took place in France, but it
fired the imagination of men far beyond the French
borders.  In England there was widespread discontent.  So long as the great Napoleonic wars
lasted the burden of taxation was very heavy, and
so soon as they were over there was terrible distress
in all the trades which had been inflated by them.
Parliament attempted to deal with the discontent
by passing severely repressive measures, but then
Parliament did not represent the great body of
working people.  Hence there were riots in the
East of England and in London, and riots in the
Midlands and in the North.  At length came the
great Reform Act of 1832, bringing social peace in
its train since by it the people were able at last to
make their voice heard and their influence felt

in the affairs of the nation. But by that time the
leaders in the National Church were either despised
or hated, for in the fierce struggles of the previous
forty years for political liberty they had been far
too seldom on the side of the people, and it was
natural that when at length the people triumphed
they should have but little regard for a Church
which had so often opposed their aims. It was in
fact regarded as impossible that the National
Church would be allowed to keep its position for
many more years. Yet once again it showed an
astonishing power of revival, facing boldly the
fierce opposition of its estranged members and
making greater claims than ever to their allegiance.

The spirit of the time was manifested in an
attempt made by the Government which came in
after the passing of the Reform Bill to suppress ten
of the Irish Bishoprics, as though the Church were a
mere department of State to be dealt with according to the caprice of a temporary majority.
Against this cynical plan John Keble, the revered
author of the 'Christian Year,' protested in the
famous Assize Sermon which he preached at
Oxford on Sunday, July 14, 1833; and it was
this sermon which was always regarded by Newman
as the origin of the religious revival which is now

generally known as the Oxford Movement. The first definite step, however, in the way of organization was taken at Hadleigh in Suffolk, where the Rector, the Rev. H. J. Rose, a Cambridge man, had called together a few High Church clergymen, and with them had resolved ' to fight for the Apostolical Succession and the integrity of the Prayer-Book.' It was the revival again of the old Laudian teaching of the seventeenth century with its assertion of the Church's position as a Divine institution possessed of the right to decree its own services and ceremonies. Shortly after this meeting at Hadleigh John Henry Newman, who was then Vicar of the University Church at Oxford, began the writing of the ' Tracts for the Times,' so that these views with which he entirely sympathized might be made more widely known ; and at the same time he began to use his pulpit also for the same purpose.

In the writing of the tracts Newman was aided by Keble, Pusey, and others, and this literary side of the movement lasted till 1841, when Newman published the famous ' Tract 90 ' in which he declared that the Thirty-nine Articles were not directed against Roman Catholic doctrine as rightly understood, but only against the popular misconceptions

26

of it. This Tract produced a storm of opposition, and at the request of the Bishop of Oxford of the time the Tracts were thereupon discontinued. From that moment Newman ceased to be the real leader of the movement, although he was not formally received into the Roman Catholic Communion until four years later. His place was taken by Pusey, who was then, and for more than forty years afterwards, one of the Canons of Christ Church, and Pusey's influence was so great that 'Puseyism' came to be the common name for the movement. Yet it was not until this new leader was made to suffer persecution that the cause can be said to have attracted the notice of the country generally. In 1843 Pusey preached a sermon on the Holy Eucharist which led to his being suspended from preaching for three years. As a result the sermon was on sale everywhere, and Pusey himself became the recognized exponent of the Catholic position of the English Church. In every department of the controversy he exercised a unique influence; by his clear statement of the doctrine of the National Church on the question of Baptismal Regeneration he kept many a man from seceding to Rome; he taught the Real Presence of Christ in the Holy Eucharist; and through his influence the practice of Confession within the Church of England was revived.

The results of this movement have been even so far exceedingly great. Reverence for the Church as a Divine institution has produced a reverence for all things connected with it ; the building of new churches and the restoration of old ones have gone on apace, and the worship within them has once again much of the dignity and beauty which were associated with it in pre-Reformation times. Even the form of the new buildings is indicative of the great changes which the Oxford Movement has produced in the teaching of the Church as a whole ; for in them it is always the sanctuary with its Holy Table which is most prominent, while the galleries, which were suitable indeed for theological lecture-halls but not for places of worship, have disappeared.

But the movement is doing more than that. In response to the longing of men in these latter days for a real brotherhood of man, it is teaching the world to see that membership in the Church implies that brotherhood, since the Church is an organization founded by the great Head Himself for the very purpose of providing the means by which each several member shall be able to obtain the Divine grace to fulfil the better his duty to the whole body.

The Church can indeed boast of a record of which, in spite of its many sad pages, its members may be justly proud ; but there is a juster reason still for pride in the fact that it is striving to-day to make all men realize that fellowship with Christ means fellowship one with another.

# INDEX

Abbot, Archbishop, 122, 134
Aidan, S., 16
Alban, S., 3
Alfred, King, 19
Andrewes, Lancelot, 123, 127, 139, 167
Anne of Bohemia, 71
Anne, Queen, 175
Anselm, Archbishop, 94
Augustine, 10, 11

Bancroft, Archbishop, 122, 125
Becket, Thomas, Archbishop, 33, 94
Bellarmine, 128
Bertha, Queen, 10
Bilney, 115
Blair, Dr., 173
Boleyn, Anne, 84, 91, 94, 115
Boniface VIII., Pope, 51
Boniface of Savoy, Archbishop, 42
Bonner, Bishop, 129
Bray, Dr., 171, 173
Bucer, Martin, 115
Burnell, Robert, 46
Burnet, Gilbert, Bishop, 164, 168
Butler, Bishop, 191

Calvin, 124
Charles I., 80, 131, 142, 151
　　　　II., 145, 151, 188
　　　　V., the Emperor, 88, 116
Cherry, Francis, 178
Clement V., Pope, 54
Colet, John, 75
Columba, S., 15

Columbus, 77
Compton, Bishop, 156
Cranmer, Thomas, Archbishop, 90
Cromwell, Oliver, 141
Cromwell, Thomas, 96

Dodwell, Henry, 178
Dominic, 43
Dunstan, S., 20, 22

Eadbold, Archbishop, 13
Edmund, King of East Anglia, 19
Edward I., 46
　　　　VI., 102, 162, 166
Edwin, King of Northumbria, 13
Elizabeth, Queen, 113, 166
Ethelbert of Kent, 10
Ethelburga, 13
Ethelfrith, 15
Ethelwold, Bishop, 21

Fisher, Bishop, 95
Fletcher, John William, 193
Francis of Assisi, 43

Gaunt, John of, 62, 113
George I., 163, 179
　　　　II., 163
　　　　III., 169
German, S., 4, 5
Goth, Bertrand de, 54
Gregory the Great, Pope, 9, 14
　　　　XIII., Pope, 118
Grey, John de, Bishop, 38
Grosseteste, Robert, Bishop, 45
Gualo, Papal Legate, 41

Henrietta Maria, Queen, 131
Henry I., 28, 32
    II., 31
    III., 41
    V., 67
    VI., 67
    VII., 82
    VIII., 80, 82, 166
Hildebrand, Pope, 25
Hoadly, Benjamin, Bishop, 181, 184
Holywood, 129
Honorius III., Pope, 41
Hooker, Richard, 123, 125, 139, 167
Horneck, Anthony, 178
Huss, 69

Innocent III., Pope, 38
Isidore, Decretals of, 30

James I., 120
    II., 80, 153, 161
Jeffreys, Judge, 156
Jerome of Prague, 71
Jewel, Bishop, 123, 124
John, King, 36
Joseph of Arimathea, 2
Justus, 13

Katharine, Queen, 81, 87, 90
Keble, John, 200
Ken, Thomas, Bishop, 179
Kettlewell, John, 178
Knox, John, 103, 124

Langland, 59
Langton, Stephen, 36, 40, 42, 94
Latimer, 115
Laud, Archbishop, 134, 167, 172, 184, 201
Leo X., Pope, 75
Lingard, John, 130
Lloyd, Bishop, 179
Louis VIII., King of France, 40
    XIV., King of France, 160
Lupus, S., 4, 5
Luther, 85

Macaulay, Zachery, 197
Mainwaring, Roger, 133
Mary, Queen, 109, 146, 166
Mary, Queen of Scotland, 114
Monmouth, Duke of, 154
Montague, Richard, 132
More, Sir Thomas, 75, 95

Nelson, Robert, 178
Newman, Cardinal, 200, 201
Newton, John, 194
Northumberland, Protector, 102, 108, 146
Nottingham, Earl of, 130

Offa, King of Mercia, 22
Oswald, 15
Oswald, S., 15
Oswy, 17

Pandolph, Papal Legate, 40
Parker, Matthew, Archbishop, 115, 129
Paul III., Pope, 95
Paulinus, 14
Peckham, John, Archbishop, 47
Pelagius, 4
Philip Augustus, King of France, 39
Philip II., King of Spain, 110
Pius IV., Pope, 117, 130
    V., Pope, 117, 130
Pusey, 201, 202

Reynolds, Walter, Archbishop, 56
Richard II., 70
Rose, Rev. H. J., 201

Sacheverell, Dr., 176
Sancroft, Archbishop, 157, 162
Sibthorpe, Dr., 132
Somerset, Protector, 102
Stapledon, Bishop, 57
Stephen of Blois, 31, 35
Stephen, James, 196

Tenison, Archbishop, 165, 174
Tertullian, 2

Theodore, Archbishop, 18
Thornton, Henry, 196
Tillotson, John, Archbishop, 164
Travers, Evening Lecturer at the
    Temple, 125

Venn, Henry, 195
Venn, John, 195
Vortigern, 7

Walpole, Prime Minister, 180
Warham, William, Archbishop, 75
Wesley, Charles, 189

Wesley, John, 189, 190
Wesley, Samuel, 171, 188
Whitefield, George, 189, 190
Whitgift, Archbishop, 119, 122
Whiting, Richard, Abbot, 99
Wilberforce, William, 196, 197,
    198
Wilfrid, Bishop, 22
William I., 25, 26
    III., 118, 158, 160, 167,
        175, 177
Winchelsea, Archbishop, 51, 52,
    94
Wycliffe, 61, 69

THE END

BILLING AND SONS, LTD., PRINTERS, GUILDFORD

MONROE.

Printed in Great Britain
by Amazon